Having Fun with Bibl

Having Fun with Bibl
By CL Gammon and Kim Gammon

Having Fun with Bible Facts, Trivia & Quotes

Text Copyright © 2018, by CL Gammon and Kim Gammon, All Rights Reserved

Having Fun with Bible Facts, Trivia & Quotes

For our children, Amy and Justin, and our granddaughters, Jayci, and Sapphira

Table of Contents

Introduction: 1
Facts, Trivia & Quotes: 4
Conclusion: 116
About the Authors: 117
Other Books by CL Gammon: 118

Introduction

The best way to get anyone – of any age – to learn is to make learning fun; make learning into a game. When we decided to write this book, we determined to try to make it as much fun and as interesting as possible. Thus, we decided to go with a "Question and Answer" format to encourage others to read the scripture as if they were playing a game.

Admittedly, almost everyone knows the answers to some of the questions presented here. However, except for ardent students of the Bible, readers will find some of the questions very challenging. Not to fear, however, we have included both the answers to the questions and the scripture containing the answers directly after the questions.

The scripture we include is often a little broader than what is absolutely required to answer the questions. We feel this is necessary to give the full scope of the events connected with the questions. Thus, the reader will be able get a fuller sense of the intent of the scripture.

In addition, we also have scattered a few facts about the Bible among the questions. We have also sprinkled a few famous quotes about Bible in the body of this book. We hope that the facts and the quotes will add to the fun.

We believe it is our mission to encourage others to read and learn about the Bible. That being the case, we have avoided doctrinal questions and issues. We are not promoting any specific sect and it is not our goal to challenge anyone's beliefs. We only desire to make Bible reading a little more interesting and a little more pleasurable for everyone.

A large percentage of this little book consists of quotes taken directly from the Bible. We have quoted the scripture exactly as it appears in the Bible and we have not changed any spellings, etc.

After much debate, we decided to quote from the King James Version of the Bible. The primary reason for this is that almost everyone who is acquainted with the Bible is aware of the King James Version. Beyond that, the King James Version is in Public Domain and is, therefore, the most readily available and the least expensive version of the Bible available. Thus, if the reader wants a Bible, he can obtain a copy of the King James Version easily and cheaply. Beyond that, the King James Version is a beautiful piece of poetry.

We have generally only included one biblical source in answering the questions presented in this book. Of course, there are often several sources available, but we saw no reason to be redundant. We do encourage you to seek out the other biblical sources relating to the answers to the questions presented here.

We have tried to the best of our ability to be accurate in everything in this book. If, however, there is a stray error in it, please contact us by email at clgammon@hotmail.com and provide us with the correction.

Having Fun with Bible Facts, Trivia & Quotes

Again, it is our hope that that everyone that reads this book will enjoy it. If readers learn a little as well, that will be great too!

Facts, Trivia & Quotes

Question: The river flowing out of Eden formed how many other rivers?

Answer: 4 (Pishon, Gihon, Hiddekel (Tigris), and Euphrates)

Reference: Genesis 2:10-14

(Genesis 2:10-14)

[10] And a river went out of Eden to water the garden; and from thence it was parted, and became into four heads.

[11] The name of the first is Pison: that is it which compasseth the whole land of Havilah, where there is gold;

[12] And the gold of that land is good: there is bdellium and the onyx stone.

[13] And the name of the second river is Gihon: the same is it that compasseth the whole land of Ethiopia.

[14] And the name of the third river is Hiddekel: that is it which goeth toward the east of Assyria. And the fourth river is Euphrates.

Question: What were the two animals in the Old Testament that spoke to humans?

Answer: A serpent and a donkey

References: Genesis 3:1-5 and Numbers 22:21-31

(Genesis 3:1-5)

[1.] Now the serpent was more subtil than any beast of the field which the Lord God had made. And he said unto the woman, Yea, hath God said, Ye shall not eat of every tree of the garden?

[2] And the woman said unto the serpent, We may eat of the fruit of the trees of the garden:

[3] But of the fruit of the tree which is in the midst of the garden, God hath said, Ye shall not eat of it, neither shall ye touch it, lest ye die.

[4] And the serpent said unto the woman, Ye shall not surely die:

[5] For God doth know that in the day ye eat thereof, then your eyes shall be opened, and ye shall be as gods, knowing good and evil.

(Numbers 22:21-31)

[21] And Balaam rose up in the morning, and saddled his ass, and went with the princes of Moab.

[22] And God's anger was kindled because he went: and the angel of the Lord stood in the way for an adversary against him. Now he was riding upon his ass, and his two servants were with him.

[23] And the ass saw the angel of the Lord standing in the way, and his sword drawn in his hand: and the ass turned aside out of the

way, and went into the field: and Balaam smote the ass, to turn her into the way.

[24] But the angel of the Lord stood in a path of the vineyards, a wall being on this side, and a wall on that side.

[25] And when the ass saw the angel of the Lord, she thrust herself unto the wall, and crushed Balaam's foot against the wall: and he smote her again.

[26] And the angel of the Lord went further, and stood in a narrow place, where was no way to turn either to the right hand or to the left.

[27] And when the ass saw the angel of the Lord, she fell down under Balaam: and Balaam's anger was kindled, and he smote the ass with a staff.

[28] And the Lord opened the mouth of the ass, and she said unto Balaam, What have I done unto thee, that thou hast smitten me these three times?

[29] And Balaam said unto the ass, Because thou hast mocked me: I would there were a sword in mine hand, for now would I kill thee.

[30] And the ass said unto Balaam, Am not I thine ass, upon which thou hast ridden ever since I was thine unto this day? was I ever wont to do so unto thee? and he said, Nay.

[31] Then the Lord opened the eyes of Balaam, and he saw the angel of the Lord standing in the way, and his sword drawn in his hand: and he bowed down his head, and fell flat on his face.

Question: What were the people building when God confused their language?

Answer: The Tower of Babel

Reference: Genesis 11:1-9

(Genesis 11:1-9)

[1] And the whole earth was of one language, and of one speech.

[2] And it came to pass, as they journeyed from the east, that they found a plain in the land of Shinar; and they dwelt there.

[3] And they said one to another, Go to, let us make brick, and burn them thoroughly. And they had brick for stone, and slime had they for morter.

[4] And they said, Go to, let us build us a city and a tower, whose top may reach unto heaven; and let us make us a name, lest we be scattered abroad upon the face of the whole earth.

[5] And the Lord came down to see the city and the tower, which the children of men builded.

[6] And the Lord said, Behold, the people is one, and they have all one language; and this they begin to do: and now nothing will be restrained from them, which they have imagined to do.

(7) Go to, let us go down, and there confound their language, that they may not understand one another's speech.

(8) So the Lord scattered them abroad from thence upon the face of all the earth: and they left off to build the city.

(9) Therefore is the name of it called Babel; because the Lord did there confound the language of all the earth: and from thence did the Lord scatter them abroad upon the face of all the earth.

Question: What is the sign of the covenant between God and Abraham?

Answer: Male Circumcision

Reference: Genesis 17:9-14

(Genesis 17:9-14)

[9] And God said unto Abraham, Thou shalt keep my covenant therefore, thou, and thy seed after thee in their generations.

[10] This is my covenant, which ye shall keep, between me and you and thy seed after thee; Every man child among you shall be circumcised.

[11] And ye shall circumcise the flesh of your foreskin; and it shall be a token of the covenant betwixt me and you.

[12] And he that is eight days old shall be circumcised among you, every man child in your generations, he that is born in the house, or bought with money of any stranger, which is not of thy seed.

[13] He that is born in thy house, and he that is bought with thy money, must needs be

circumcised: and my covenant shall be in your flesh for an everlasting covenant.

[14] And the uncircumcised man child whose flesh of his foreskin is not circumcised, that soul shall be cut off from his people; he hath broken my covenant.

Question: How old was Isaac when he married?

Answer: 40

Reference: Genesis 25:20

(Genesis 25:20)

[20] And Isaac was forty years old when he took Rebekah to wife, the daughter of Bethuel the Syrian of Padanaram, the sister to Laban the Syrian.

Question: Who sold his birthright to his brother for a meal?

Answer: Esau

Reference: Genesis 25:27-34

(Genesis 25:27-34)

[27] And the boys grew: and Esau was a cunning hunter, a man of the field; and Jacob was a plain man, dwelling in tents.

[28] And Isaac loved Esau, because he did eat of his venison: but Rebekah loved Jacob.

[29] And Jacob sod pottage: and Esau came from the field, and he was faint:

[30] And Esau said to Jacob, Feed me, I pray thee, with that same red pottage; for I am faint: therefore was his name called Edom.

[31] And Jacob said, Sell me this day thy birthright.

[32] And Esau said, Behold, I am at the point to die: and what profit shall this birthright do to me?

[33] And Jacob said, Swear to me this day; and he sware unto him: and he sold his birthright unto Jacob.

[34] Then Jacob gave Esau bread and pottage of lentiles; and he did eat and drink, and rose up, and went his way: thus Esau despised his birthright.

Question: How old was Esau when he married.

Answer: 40

Reference: Genesis 26:34-35

(Genesis 26:34-35)

[34] And Esau was forty years old when he took to wife Judith the daughter of Beeri the Hittite, and Bashemath the daughter of Elon the Hittite:

[35] Which were a grief of mind unto Isaac and to Rebekah.

Question: Where did Jacob sleep and dream of Jacob's Ladder?

Answer: Bethel

Reference: Genesis 28:10-19

(Genesis 28:10-19)

[10] And Jacob went out from Beersheba, and went toward Haran.

[11] And he lighted upon a certain place, and tarried there all night, because the sun was set; and he took of the stones of that place, and put them for his pillows, and lay down in that place to sleep.

[12] And he dreamed, and behold a ladder set up on the earth, and the top of it reached to heaven: and behold the angels of God ascending and descending on it.

[13] And, behold, the Lord stood above it, and said, I am the Lord God of Abraham thy father, and the God of Isaac: the land whereon thou liest, to thee will I give it, and to thy seed;

[14] And thy seed shall be as the dust of the earth, and thou shalt spread abroad to the west, and to the east, and to the north, and to the south: and in thee and in thy seed shall all the families of the earth be blessed.

[15] And, behold, I am with thee, and will keep thee in all places whither thou goest, and will bring thee again into this land; for I will not leave thee, until I have done that which I have spoken to thee of.

[16] And Jacob awaked out of his sleep, and he said, Surely the Lord is in this place; and I knew it not.

[17] And he was afraid, and said, How dreadful is this place! this is none other but the house of God, and this is the gate of heaven.

[18] And Jacob rose up early in the morning, and took the stone that he had put for his pillows, and set it up for a pillar, and poured oil upon the top of it.

[19] And he called the name of that place Bethel: but the name of that city was called Luz at the first.

Bible Fact: The King James Version of the Bible contains 788,258 words, 31,102 verses, 1,189 chapters, and 66 books. (The Old Testament has 39 books and the New Testament has 29 books).

Question: What were the ten plagues God visited upon Egypt?

Answer:

(1) Plague of water turned to blood

(2) Plague of frogs

(3) Plague of lice

(4) Plague of flies

(5) Plague on cattle

(6) Plague of boils

(7) Plague of hail

(8) Plague of locusts

(9) Plague of darkness

(10) Plague of death of the firstborn

Reference: Exodus 7:14-25; Exodus 8:1-6; 16-17; 20-24; Exodus 9:1-10, 18-26, Exodus 10:3-15, 21-26; 11:1, 4-7; 12:12, 23, 29-30

(Exodus 7:14-25)

[14] And the Lord said unto Moses, Pharaoh's heart is hardened, he refuseth to let the people go.

[15] Get thee unto Pharaoh in the morning; lo, he goeth out unto the water; and thou shalt stand by the river's brink against he come; and the rod which was turned to a serpent shalt thou take in thine hand.

[16] And thou shalt say unto him, The Lord God of the Hebrews hath sent me unto thee, saying, Let my people go, that they may serve me in the wilderness: and, behold, hitherto thou wouldest not hear.

[17] Thus saith the Lord, In this thou shalt know that I am the Lord: behold, I will smite with the rod that is in mine hand upon the waters which are in the river, and they shall be turned to blood.

[18] And the fish that is in the river shall die, and the river shall stink; and the Egyptians shall lothe to drink of the water of the river.

[19] And the Lord spake unto Moses, Say unto Aaron, Take thy rod, and stretch out thine hand upon the waters of Egypt, upon their streams, upon their rivers, and upon their ponds, and upon all their pools of water, that they may become blood; and that there

may be blood throughout all the land of Egypt, both in vessels of wood, and in vessels of stone.

[20] And Moses and Aaron did so, as the Lord commanded; and he lifted up the rod, and smote the waters that were in the river, in the sight of Pharaoh, and in the sight of his servants; and all the waters that were in the river were turned to blood.

[21] And the fish that was in the river died; and the river stank, and the Egyptians could not drink of the water of the river; and there was blood throughout all the land of Egypt.

[22] And the magicians of Egypt did so with their enchantments: and Pharaoh's heart was hardened, neither did he hearken unto them; as the Lord had said.

[23] And Pharaoh turned and went into his house, neither did he set his heart to this also.

[24] And all the Egyptians digged round about the river for water to drink; for they could not drink of the water of the river.

[25] And seven days were fulfilled, after that the Lord had smitten the river.

(Exodus 8:1-6, 16-17, 20-24)

[1] And the Lord spake unto Moses, Go unto Pharaoh, and say unto him, Thus saith the Lord, Let my people go, that they may serve me.

[2] And if thou refuse to let them go, behold, I will smite all thy borders with frogs:

[3] And the river shall bring forth frogs abundantly, which shall go up and come into

thine house, and into thy bedchamber, and upon thy bed, and into the house of thy servants, and upon thy people, and into thine ovens, and into thy kneading troughs:

[4] And the frogs shall come up both on thee, and upon thy people, and upon all thy servants.

[5] And the Lord spake unto Moses, Say unto Aaron, Stretch forth thine hand with thy rod over the streams, over the rivers, and over the ponds, and cause frogs to come up upon the land of Egypt.

[16] And the Lord said unto Moses, Say unto Aaron, Stretch out thy rod, and smite the dust of the land, that it may become lice throughout all the land of Egypt.

[17] And they did so; for Aaron stretched out his hand with his rod, and smote the dust of the earth, and it became lice in man, and in beast; all the dust of the land became lice throughout all the land of Egypt.

[20] And the Lord said unto Moses, Rise up early in the morning, and stand before Pharaoh; lo, he cometh forth to the water; and say unto him, Thus saith the Lord, Let my people go, that they may serve me.

[21] Else, if thou wilt not let my people go, behold, I will send swarms of flies upon thee, and upon thy servants, and upon thy people, and into thy houses: and the houses of the Egyptians shall be full of swarms of flies, and also the ground whereon they are.

[22] And I will sever in that day the land of Goshen, in which my people dwell, that no swarms of flies shall be there; to the end thou mayest know that I am the Lord in the midst of the earth.

[23] And I will put a division between my people and thy people: to morrow shall this sign be.

[24] And the Lord did so; and there came a grievous swarm of flies into the house of Pharaoh, and into his servants' houses, and into all the land of Egypt: the land was corrupted by reason of the swarm of flies.

(Exodus 9:1-10, 18-26)

[1] Then the Lord said unto Moses, Go in unto Pharaoh, and tell him, Thus saith the Lord God of the Hebrews, Let my people go, that they may serve me.

[2] For if thou refuse to let them go, and wilt hold them still,

[3] Behold, the hand of the Lord is upon thy cattle which is in the field, upon the horses, upon the asses, upon the camels, upon the oxen, and upon the sheep: there shall be a very grievous murrain.

[4] And the Lord shall sever between the cattle of Israel and the cattle of Egypt: and there shall nothing die of all that is the children's of Israel.

[5] And the Lord appointed a set time, saying, To morrow the Lord shall do this thing in the land.

[6] And the Lord did that thing on the morrow, and all the cattle of Egypt died: but of the cattle of the children of Israel died not one.

[7] And Pharaoh sent, and, behold, there was not one of the cattle of the Israelites dead. And the heart of Pharaoh was hardened, and he did not let the people go.

[8] And the Lord said unto Moses and unto Aaron, Take to you handfuls of ashes of the furnace, and let Moses sprinkle it toward the heaven in the sight of Pharaoh.

[9] And it shall become small dust in all the land of Egypt, and shall be a boil breaking forth with blains upon man, and upon beast, throughout all the land of Egypt.

[10] And they took ashes of the furnace, and stood before Pharaoh; and Moses sprinkled it up toward heaven; and it became a boil breaking forth with blains upon man, and upon beast.

[18] Behold, to morrow about this time I will cause it to rain a very grievous hail, such as hath not been in Egypt since the foundation thereof even until now.

[19] Send therefore now, and gather thy cattle, and all that thou hast in the field; for upon every man and beast which shall be found in the field, and shall not be brought home, the hail shall come down upon them, and they shall die.

[20] He that feared the word of the Lord among the servants of Pharaoh made his servants and his cattle flee into the houses:

[21] And he that regarded not the word of the Lord left his servants and his cattle in the field.

[22] And the Lord said unto Moses, Stretch forth thine hand toward heaven, that there may be hail in all the land of Egypt, upon man, and upon beast, and upon every herb of the field, throughout the land of Egypt.

[23] And Moses stretched forth his rod toward heaven: and the Lord sent thunder and hail, and the fire ran along upon the ground; and the Lord rained hail upon the land of Egypt.

[24] So there was hail, and fire mingled with the hail, very grievous, such as there was none like it in all the land of Egypt since it became a nation.

[25] And the hail smote throughout all the land of Egypt all that was in the field, both man and beast; and the hail smote every herb of the field, and brake every tree of the field.

[26] Only in the land of Goshen, where the children of Israel were, was there no hail.

(Exodus 10:3-15, 21-26)

[3] And Moses and Aaron came in unto Pharaoh, and said unto him, Thus saith the Lord God of the Hebrews, How long wilt thou refuse to humble thyself before me? let my people go, that they may serve me.

[4] Else, if thou refuse to let my people go, behold, to morrow will I bring the locusts into thy coast:

[5] And they shall cover the face of the earth, that one cannot be able to see the earth: and they shall eat the residue of that which is escaped, which remaineth unto you from the hail, and shall eat every tree which groweth for you out of the field:

[6] And they shall fill thy houses, and the houses of all thy servants, and the houses of all the Egyptians; which neither thy fathers, nor thy fathers' fathers have seen, since the day that they were upon the earth unto this day. And he turned himself, and went out from Pharaoh.

[7] And Pharaoh's servants said unto him, How long shall this man be a snare unto us? let the men go, that they may serve the Lord their God: knowest thou not yet that Egypt is destroyed?

[8] And Moses and Aaron were brought again unto Pharaoh: and he said unto them, Go, serve the Lord your God: but who are they that shall go?

[9] And Moses said, We will go with our young and with our old, with our sons and with our daughters, with our flocks and with our herds will we go; for we must hold a feast unto the Lord.

[10] And he said unto them, Let the Lord be so with you, as I will let you go, and your little ones: look to it; for evil is before you.

[11] Not so: go now ye that are men, and serve the Lord; for that ye did desire. And they were driven out from Pharaoh's presence.

[12] And the Lord said unto Moses, Stretch out thine hand over the land of Egypt for the locusts, that they may come up upon the land of Egypt, and eat every herb of the land, even all that the hail hath left.

[13] And Moses stretched forth his rod over the land of Egypt, and the Lord brought an east wind upon the land all that day, and all that night; and when it was morning, the east wind brought the locusts.

[14] And the locust went up over all the land of Egypt, and rested in all the coasts of Egypt: very grievous were they; before them there were no such locusts as they, neither after them shall be such.

[15] For they covered the face of the whole earth, so that the land was darkened; and they did eat every herb of the land, and all the fruit of the trees which the hail had left: and there remained not any green thing in the trees, or in the herbs of the field, through all the land of Egypt.

[21] And the Lord said unto Moses, Stretch out thine hand toward heaven, that there may be darkness over the land of Egypt, even darkness which may be felt.

[22] And Moses stretched forth his hand toward heaven; and there was a thick darkness in all the land of Egypt three days:

[23] They saw not one another, neither rose any from his place for three days: but all the children of Israel had light in their dwellings.

[24] And Pharaoh called unto Moses, and said, Go ye, serve the Lord; only let your flocks and your herds be stayed: let your little ones also go with you.

[25] And Moses said, Thou must give us also sacrifices and burnt offerings, that we may sacrifice unto the Lord our God.

[26] Our cattle also shall go with us; there shall not an hoof be left behind; for thereof must we take to serve the Lord our God; and we know not with what we must serve the Lord, until we come thither.

(Exodus 11: 1, 4-7)

[1] And the Lord said unto Moses, Yet will I bring one plague more upon Pharaoh, and upon Egypt; afterwards he will let you go hence: when he shall let you go, he shall surely thrust you out hence altogether.

[4] And Moses said, Thus saith the Lord, About midnight will I go out into the midst of Egypt:

[5] And all the firstborn in the land of Egypt shall die, from the first born of Pharaoh that sitteth upon his throne, even unto the firstborn of the maidservant that is behind the mill; and all the firstborn of beasts.

[6] And there shall be a great cry throughout all the land of Egypt, such as there was none like it, nor shall be like it any more.

[7] But against any of the children of Israel shall not a dog move his tongue, against man or beast: that ye may know how that the Lord doth put a difference between the Egyptians and Israel.

(Exodus 12:12, 23, 29-30)

[12] For I will pass through the land of Egypt this night, and will smite all the firstborn in the land of Egypt, both man and beast; and against all the gods of Egypt I will execute judgment: I am the Lord.

[23] For the Lord will pass through to smite the Egyptians; and when he seeth the blood upon the lintel, and on the two side posts, the Lord will pass over the door, and will not suffer the destroyer to come in unto your houses to smite you.

[29] And it came to pass, that at midnight the Lord smote all the firstborn in the land of Egypt, from the firstborn of Pharaoh that sat on his throne unto the firstborn of the captive that was in the dungeon; and all the firstborn of cattle.

[30] And Pharaoh rose up in the night, he, and all his servants, and all the Egyptians; and there was a great cry in Egypt; for there was not a house where there was not one dead.

Quote: "Visit many good books, but live in the Bible." – Charles Spurgeon

Question: How did Moses make the bitter waters of Marah drinkable?

Answer: He threw wood into the water

Reference: Exodus 15:22-26

(Exodus 15:22-26)

[22] So Moses brought Israel from the Red sea, and they went out into the wilderness of Shur; and they went three days in the wilderness, and found no water.

[23] And when they came to Marah, they could not drink of the waters of Marah, for they were bitter: therefore the name of it was called Marah.

[24] And the people murmured against Moses, saying, What shall we drink?

[25] And he cried unto the Lord; and the Lord shewed him a tree, which when he had cast into the waters, the waters were made sweet: there he made for them a statute and an ordinance, and there he proved them,

[26] And said, If thou wilt diligently hearken to the voice of the Lord thy God, and wilt do that which is right in his sight, and wilt give ear to his commandments, and keep all his statutes, I will put none of these diseases upon thee, which I have brought upon the Egyptians: for I am the Lord that healeth thee.

Question: How did Moses assure victory against the Amalekites?

Answer: He held up his hands

Reference: Exodus 17:8-13

(Exodus 17:8-13)

[8] Then came Amalek, and fought with Israel in Rephidim.

[9] And Moses said unto Joshua, Choose us out men, and go out, fight with Amalek: to morrow I will stand on the top of the hill with the rod of God in mine hand.

[10] So Joshua did as Moses had said to him, and fought with Amalek: and Moses, Aaron, and Hur went up to the top of the hill.

[11] And it came to pass, when Moses held up his hand, that Israel prevailed: and when he let down his hand, Amalek prevailed.

[12] But Moses hands were heavy; and they took a stone, and put it under him, and he sat thereon; and Aaron and Hur stayed up his hands, the one on the one side, and the other on the other side; and his hands were steady until the going down of the sun.

[13] And Joshua discomfited Amalek and his people with the edge of the sword.

Question: Who was Israel's first High Priest?

Answer: Aaron

Reference: Exodus 28

(Exodus 28)

[1]. And take thou unto thee Aaron thy brother, and his sons with him, from among

the children of Israel, that he may minister unto me in the priest's office, even Aaron, Nadab and Abihu, Eleazar and Ithamar, Aaron's sons.

[2] And thou shalt make holy garments for Aaron thy brother for glory and for beauty.

[3] And thou shalt speak unto all that are wise hearted, whom I have filled with the spirit of wisdom, that they may make Aaron's garments to consecrate him, that he may minister unto me in the priest's office.

[4] And these are the garments which they shall make; a breastplate, and an ephod, and a robe, and a broidered coat, a mitre, and a girdle: and they shall make holy garments for Aaron thy brother, and his sons, that he may minister unto me in the priest's office.

[5] And they shall take gold, and blue, and purple, and scarlet, and fine linen.

[6] And they shall make the ephod of gold, of blue, and of purple, of scarlet, and fine twined linen, with cunning work.

[7] It shall have the two shoulderpieces thereof joined at the two edges thereof; and so it shall be joined together.

[8] And the curious girdle of the ephod, which is upon it, shall be of the same, according to the work thereof; even of gold, of blue, and purple, and scarlet, and fine twined linen.

[9] And thou shalt take two onyx stones, and grave on them the names of the children of Israel:

[10] Six of their names on one stone, and the other six names of the rest on the other stone, according to their birth.

[11] With the work of an engraver in stone, like the engravings of a signet, shalt thou engrave the two stones with the names of the children of Israel: thou shalt make them to be set in ouches of gold.

[12] And thou shalt put the two stones upon the shoulders of the ephod for stones of memorial unto the children of Israel: and Aaron shall bear their names before the Lord upon his two shoulders for a memorial.

[13] And thou shalt make ouches of gold;

[14] And two chains of pure gold at the ends; of wreathen work shalt thou make them, and fasten the wreathen chains to the ouches.

[15] And thou shalt make the breastplate of judgment with cunning work; after the work of the ephod thou shalt make it; of gold, of blue, and of purple, and of scarlet, and of fine twined linen, shalt thou make it.

[16] Foursquare it shall be being doubled; a span shall be the length thereof, and a span shall be the breadth thereof.

[17] And thou shalt set in it settings of stones, even four rows of stones: the first row shall be a sardius, a topaz, and a carbuncle: this shall be the first row.

[18] And the second row shall be an emerald, a sapphire, and a diamond.

[19] And the third row a ligure, an agate, and an amethyst.

[20] And the fourth row a beryl, and an onyx, and a jasper: they shall be set in gold in their inclosings.

[21] And the stones shall be with the names of the children of Israel, twelve, according to their names, like the engravings of a signet; every one with his name shall they be according to the twelve tribes.

[22] And thou shalt make upon the breastplate chains at the ends of wreathen work of pure gold.

[23] And thou shalt make upon the breastplate two rings of gold, and shalt put the two rings on the two ends of the breastplate.

[24] And thou shalt put the two wreathen chains of gold in the two rings which are on the ends of the breastplate.

[25] And the other two ends of the two wreathen chains thou shalt fasten in the two ouches, and put them on the shoulderpieces of the ephod before it.

[26] And thou shalt make two rings of gold, and thou shalt put them upon the two ends of the breastplate in the border thereof, which is in the side of the ephod inward.

[27] And two other rings of gold thou shalt make, and shalt put them on the two sides of the ephod underneath, toward the forepart thereof, over against the other coupling thereof, above the curious girdle of the ephod.

[28] And they shall bind the breastplate by the rings thereof unto the rings of the ephod

with a lace of blue, that it may be above the curious girdle of the ephod, and that the breastplate be not loosed from the ephod.

[29] And Aaron shall bear the names of the children of Israel in the breastplate of judgment upon his heart, when he goeth in unto the holy place, for a memorial before the Lord continually.

[30] And thou shalt put in the breastplate of judgment the Urim and the Thummim; and they shall be upon Aaron's heart, when he goeth in before the Lord: and Aaron shall bear the judgment of the children of Israel upon his heart before the Lord continually.

[31] And thou shalt make the robe of the ephod all of blue.

[32] And there shall be an hole in the top of it, in the midst thereof: it shall have a binding of woven work round about the hole of it, as it were the hole of an habergeon, that it be not rent.

[33] And beneath upon the hem of it thou shalt make pomegranates of blue, and of purple, and of scarlet, round about the hem thereof; and bells of gold between them round about:

[34] A golden bell and a pomegranate, a golden bell and a pomegranate, upon the hem of the robe round about.

[35] And it shall be upon Aaron to minister: and his sound shall be heard when he goeth in unto the holy place before the Lord, and when he cometh out, that he die not.

[36] And thou shalt make a plate of pure gold, and grave upon it, like the engravings of a signet, Holiness To The Lord.

[37] And thou shalt put it on a blue lace, that it may be upon the mitre; upon the forefront of the mitre it shall be.

[38] And it shall be upon Aaron's forehead, that Aaron may bear the iniquity of the holy things, which the children of Israel shall hallow in all their holy gifts; and it shall be always upon his forehead, that they may be accepted before the Lord.

[39] And thou shalt embroider the coat of fine linen, and thou shalt make the mitre of fine linen, and thou shalt make the girdle of needlework.

[40] And for Aaron's sons thou shalt make coats, and thou shalt make for them girdles, and bonnets shalt thou make for them, for glory and for beauty.

[41] And thou shalt put them upon Aaron thy brother, and his sons with him; and shalt anoint them, and consecrate them, and sanctify them, that they may minister unto me in the priest's office.

[42] And thou shalt make them linen breeches to cover their nakedness; from the loins even unto the thighs they shall reach:

[43] And they shall be upon Aaron, and upon his sons, when they come in unto the tabernacle of the congregation, or when they come near unto the altar to minister in the holy place; that they bear not iniquity, and

die: it shall be a statute for ever unto him and his seed after him.

Question: What was the animal represented by the idol Aaron fashioned from gold for the Israelites?

Answer: A calf

Reference: Exodus 32:1-6

(Exodus 32:1-6)

[1] And when the people saw that Moses delayed to come down out of the mount, the people gathered themselves together unto Aaron, and said unto him, Up, make us gods, which shall go before us; for as for this Moses, the man that brought us up out of the land of Egypt, we wot not what is become of him.

[2] And Aaron said unto them, Break off the golden earrings, which are in the ears of your wives, of your sons, and of your daughters, and bring them unto me.

[3] And all the people brake off the golden earrings which were in their ears, and brought them unto Aaron.

[4] And he received them at their hand, and fashioned it with a graving tool, after he had made it a molten calf: and they said, These be thy gods, O Israel, which brought thee up out of the land of Egypt.

[5] And when Aaron saw it, he built an altar before it; and Aaron made proclamation, and said, To morrow is a feast to the Lord.

[6] And they rose up early on the morrow, and offered burnt offerings, and brought peace offerings; and the people sat down to eat and to drink, and rose up to play.

Question: When Moses was preparing the Israelites for their coming confrontation with the seven nations of Canaan, how large an army did he raise?

Answer: 603,550

Reference: Numbers 1:45-46

(Numbers 1:45-46)

[45] So were all those that were numbered of the children of Israel, by the house of their fathers, from twenty years old and upward, all that were able to go forth to war in Israel;

[46] Even all they that were numbered were six hundred thousand and three thousand and five hundred and fifty.

Question: What did Moses do that kept him from entering the land of Canaan?

Answer: He brought forth water from the rock by striking it twice with his rod rather than by speaking to it as God commanded.

Reference: Numbers 20:7-12

(Numbers 20:7-12)

(7) And the Lord spake unto Moses, saying,

(8) Take the rod, and gather thou the assembly together, thou, and Aaron thy brother, and speak ye unto the rock before

their eyes; and it shall give forth his water, and thou shalt bring forth to them water out of the rock: so thou shalt give the congregation and their beasts drink.

(9) And Moses took the rod from before the Lord, as he commanded him.

(10) And Moses and Aaron gathered the congregation together before the rock, and he said unto them, Hear now, ye rebels; must we fetch you water out of this rock?

(11) And Moses lifted up his hand, and with his rod he smote the rock twice: and the water came out abundantly, and the congregation drank, and their beasts also.

(12) And the Lord spake unto Moses and Aaron, Because ye believed me not, to sanctify me in the eyes of the children of Israel, therefore ye shall not bring this congregation into the land which I have given them.

Question: How many spies did Moses send out to explore the land of Canaan?

Answer: 12

Reference: Numbers 13

(Numbers 13)

[1] And the Lord spake unto Moses, saying,

[2] Send thou men, that they may search the land of Canaan, which I give unto the children of Israel: of every tribe of their fathers shall ye send a man, every one a ruler among them.

[3] And Moses by the commandment of the Lord sent them from the wilderness of Paran: all those men were heads of the children of Israel.

[4] And these were their names: of the tribe of Reuben, Shammua the son of Zaccur.

[5] Of the tribe of Simeon, Shaphat the son of Hori.

[6] Of the tribe of Judah, Caleb the son of Jephunneh.

[7] Of the tribe of Issachar, Igal the son of Joseph.

[8] Of the tribe of Ephraim, Oshea the son of Nun.

[9] Of the tribe of Benjamin, Palti the son of Raphu.

[10] Of the tribe of Zebulun, Gaddiel the son of Sodi.

[11] Of the tribe of Joseph, namely, of the tribe of Manasseh, Gaddi the son of Susi.

[12] Of the tribe of Dan, Ammiel the son of Gemalli.

[13] Of the tribe of Asher, Sethur the son of Michael.

[14] Of the tribe of Naphtali, Nahbi the son of Vophsi.

[15] Of the tribe of Gad, Geuel the son of Machi.

[16] These are the names of the men which Moses sent to spy out the land. And Moses called Oshea the son of Nun Jehoshua.

[17] And Moses sent them to spy out the land of Canaan, and said unto them, Get you up this way southward, and go up into the mountain:

[18] And see the land, what it is, and the people that dwelleth therein, whether they be strong or weak, few or many;

[19] And what the land is that they dwell in, whether it be good or bad; and what cities they be that they dwell in, whether in tents, or in strong holds;

[20] And what the land is, whether it be fat or lean, whether there be wood therein, or not. And be ye of good courage, and bring of the fruit of the land. Now the time was the time of the firstripe grapes.

[21] So they went up, and searched the land from the wilderness of Zin unto Rehob, as men come to Hamath.

[22] And they ascended by the south, and came unto Hebron; where Ahiman, Sheshai, and Talmai, the children of Anak, were. (Now Hebron was built seven years before Zoan in Egypt.)

[23] And they came unto the brook of Eshcol, and cut down from thence a branch with one cluster of grapes, and they bare it between two upon a staff; and they brought of the pomegranates, and of the figs.

[24] The place was called the brook Eshcol, because of the cluster of grapes which the children of Israel cut down from thence.

[25] And they returned from searching of the land after forty days.

[26] And they went and came to Moses, and to Aaron, and to all the congregation of the children of Israel, unto the wilderness of Paran, to Kadesh; and brought back word unto them, and unto all the congregation, and shewed them the fruit of the land.

[27] And they told him, and said, We came unto the land whither thou sentest us, and surely it floweth with milk and honey; and this is the fruit of it.

[28] Nevertheless the people be strong that dwell in the land, and the cities are walled, and very great: and moreover we saw the children of Anak there.

[29] The Amalekites dwell in the land of the south: and the Hittites, and the Jebusites, and the Amorites, dwell in the mountains: and the Canaanites dwell by the sea, and by the coast of Jordan.

[30] And Caleb stilled the people before Moses, and said, Let us go up at once, and possess it; for we are well able to overcome it.

[31] But the men that went up with him said, We be not able to go up against the people; for they are stronger than we.

[32] And they brought up an evil report of the land which they had searched unto the children of Israel, saying, The land, through which we have gone to search it, is a land that eateth up the inhabitants thereof; and all the

people that we saw in it are men of a great stature.

[33] And there we saw the giants, the sons of Anak, which come of the giants: and we were in our own sight as grasshoppers, and so we were in their sight.

Question: Who was the successor to Moses?

Answer: Joshua

Reference: Joshua 1:1-9

(Joshua 1:1-9)

[1] Now after the death of Moses the servant of the Lord it came to pass, that the Lord spake unto Joshua the son of Nun, Moses' minister, saying,

[2] Moses my servant is dead; now therefore arise, go over this Jordan, thou, and all this people, unto the land which I do give to them, even to the children of Israel.

[3] Every place that the sole of your foot shall tread upon, that have I given unto you, as I said unto Moses.

[4] From the wilderness and this Lebanon even unto the great river, the river Euphrates, all the land of the Hittites, and unto the great sea toward the going down of the sun, shall be your coast.

[5] There shall not any man be able to stand before thee all the days of thy life: as I was with Moses, so I will be with thee: I will not fail thee, nor forsake thee.

[6] Be strong and of a good courage: for unto this people shalt thou divide for an inheritance the land, which I sware unto their fathers to give them.

[7] Only be thou strong and very courageous, that thou mayest observe to do according to all the law, which Moses my servant commanded thee: turn not from it to the right hand or to the left, that thou mayest prosper withersoever thou goest.

[8] This book of the law shall not depart out of thy mouth; but thou shalt meditate therein day and night, that thou mayest observe to do according to all that is written therein: for then thou shalt make thy way prosperous, and then thou shalt have good success.

[9] Have not I commanded thee? Be strong and of a good courage; be not afraid, neither be thou dismayed: for the Lord thy God is with thee whithersoever thou goest.

Question: Who hid Joshua's spies from Jericho's king?

Answer: Rahab the harlot

Reference: Joshua 2:1-7

(Joshua 2:1-7)

[1] And Joshua the son of Nun sent out of Shittim two men to spy secretly, saying, Go view the land, even Jericho. And they went, and came into an harlot's house, named Rahab, and lodged there.

[2] And it was told the king of Jericho, saying, Behold, there came men in hither to night of the children of Israel to search out the country.

[3] And the king of Jericho sent unto Rahab, saying, Bring forth the men that are come to thee, which are entered into thine house: for they be come to search out all the country.

[4] And the woman took the two men, and hid them, and said thus, There came men unto me, but I wist not whence they were:

[5] And it came to pass about the time of shutting of the gate, when it was dark, that the men went out: whither the men went I wot not: pursue after them quickly; for ye shall overtake them.

[6] But she had brought them up to the roof of the house, and hid them with the stalks of flax, which she had laid in order upon the roof.

[7] And the men pursued after them the way to Jordan unto the fords: and as soon as they which pursued after them were gone out, they shut the gate.

Quote: "Within the covers of the Bible are the answers for all the problems men face." – Ronald Reagan

Question: On the Seventh day, how many times did Joshua's army march around Jericho before the walls of the city tumbled down?

Answer: 7

Reference: Joshua 6:2-5

(Joshua 6:2-5)

[2] And the Lord said unto Joshua, See, I have given into thine hand Jericho, and the king thereof, and the mighty men of valour.

[3] And ye shall compass the city, all ye men of war, and go round about the city once. Thus shalt thou do six days.

[4] And seven priests shall bear before the ark seven trumpets of rams' horns: and the seventh day ye shall compass the city seven times, and the priests shall blow with the trumpets.

[5] And it shall come to pass, that when they make a long blast with the ram's horn, and when ye hear the sound of the trumpet, all the people shall shout with a great shout; and the wall of the city shall fall down flat, and the people shall ascend up every man straight before him.

Question: Whom did the sun and moon stand still before?

Answer: Joshua

Reference: Joshua 10:12-13

(Joshua 10:12-13)

[12] Then spake Joshua to the Lord in the day when the Lord delivered up the Amorites before the children of Israel, and he said in the sight of Israel, Sun, stand thou still upon Gibeon; and thou, Moon, in the valley of Ajalon.

[13] And the sun stood still, and the moon stayed, until the people had avenged themselves upon their enemies. Is not this written in the book of Jasher? So the sun stood still in the midst of heaven, and hasted not to go down about a whole day.

Bible Fact: Many authors wrote portions of the Bible. The period of the writing covered about 1,500 years.

Question: Who said, ". . . as for me and my house, we will serve the Lord"?

Answer: Joshua

Reference: Joshua 24:15

(Joshua 24:15)

[15] And if it seem evil unto you to serve the Lord, choose you this day whom ye will serve; whether the gods which your fathers served that were on the other side of the flood, or the gods of the Amorites, in whose land ye dwell: but as for me and my house, we will serve the Lord.

Quote: "I never saw a useful Christian who was not a student of the Bible." – D. L. Moody

Question: How did Jael kill Sisera?

Answer: She drove a tent stake through his head with a hammer.

Reference: Judges 4:17-21

(Judges 4:17-21)

[17] Howbeit Sisera fled away on his feet to the tent of Jael the wife of Heber the Kenite: for there was peace between Jabin the king of Hazor and the house of Heber the Kenite.

[18] And Jael went out to meet Sisera, and said unto him, Turn in, my lord, turn in to me; fear not. And when he had turned in unto her into the tent, she covered him with a mantle.

[19] And he said unto her, Give me, I pray thee, a little water to drink; for I am thirsty. And she opened a bottle of milk, and gave him drink, and covered him.

[20] Again he said unto her, Stand in the door of the tent, and it shall be, when any man doth come and enquire of thee, and say, Is there any man here? that thou shalt say, No.

[21] Then Jael Heber's wife took a nail of the tent, and took an hammer in her hand, and went softly unto him, and smote the nail into his temples, and fastened it into the ground: for he was fast asleep and weary. So he died.

Question: What object did Gideon place on the ground to receive a sign from God?

Answer: A wool fleece

Reference: Judges 6:36-37

(Judges 6:36-37)

[36] And Gideon said unto God, If thou wilt save Israel by mine hand, as thou hast said,

[37] Behold, I will put a fleece of wool in the floor; and if the dew be on the fleece only, and it be dry upon all the earth beside, then shall I know that thou wilt save Israel by mine hand, as thou hast said.

Question: What was the name of the judge who vowed his daughter to the Lord as a burnt offering?

Answer: Jephthah

Reference: Judges 11:30-40

(Judges 11:30-40)

[30] And Jephthah vowed a vow unto the Lord, and said, If thou shalt without fail deliver the children of Ammon into mine hands,

[31] Then it shall be, that whatsoever cometh forth of the doors of my house to meet me, when I return in peace from the children of Ammon, shall surely be the Lord's, and I will offer it up for a burnt offering.

[32] So Jephthah passed over unto the children of Ammon to fight against them; and the Lord delivered them into his hands.

[33] And he smote them from Aroer, even till thou come to Minnith, even twenty cities, and unto the plain of the vineyards, with a very great slaughter. Thus the children of Ammon were subdued before the children of Israel.

[34] And Jephthah came to Mizpeh unto his house, and, behold, his daughter came out to

meet him with timbrels and with dances: and she was his only child; beside her he had neither son nor daughter.

[35] And it came to pass, when he saw her, that he rent his clothes, and said, Alas, my daughter! thou hast brought me very low, and thou art one of them that trouble me: for I have opened my mouth unto the Lord, and I cannot go back.

[36] And she said unto him, My father, if thou hast opened thy mouth unto the Lord, do to me according to that which hath proceeded out of thy mouth; forasmuch as the Lord hath taken vengeance for thee of thine enemies, even of the children of Ammon.

[37] And she said unto her father, Let this thing be done for me: let me alone two months, that I may go up and down upon the mountains, and bewail my virginity, I and my fellows.

[38] And he said, Go. And he sent her away for two months: and she went with her companions, and bewailed her virginity upon the mountains.

[39] And it came to pass at the end of two months, that she returned unto her father, who did with her according to his vow which he had vowed: and she knew no man. And it was a custom in Israel,

[40] That the daughters of Israel went yearly to lament the daughter of Jephthah the Gileadite four days in a year.

Question: Who ate honey out of a lion's carcass?

Answer: Samson

Reference: Judges 14:5-9

(Judges 14:5-9)

[5] Then went Samson down, and his father and his mother, to Timnath, and came to the vineyards of Timnath: and, behold, a young lion roared against him.

[6] And the Spirit of the Lord came mightily upon him, and he rent him as he would have rent a kid, and he had nothing in his hand: but he told not his father or his mother what he had done.

[7] And he went down, and talked with the woman; and she pleased Samson well.

[8] And after a time he returned to take her, and he turned aside to see the carcase of the lion: and, behold, there was a swarm of bees and honey in the carcase of the lion.

[9] And he took thereof in his hands, and went on eating, and came to his father and mother, and he gave them, and they did eat: but he told not them that he had taken the honey out of the carcase of the lion.

Question: What weapon did Samson use to kill the 1,000 Philistines at Lehi?

Answer: The jawbone of a Donkey

Reference: Judges 15:14-16

(Judges 15:14-16)

[14] And when he came unto Lehi, the Philistines shouted against him: and the Spirit of the Lord came mightily upon him, and the cords that were upon his arms became as flax that was burnt with fire, and his bands loosed from off his hands.

[15] And he found a new jawbone of an ass, and put forth his hand, and took it, and slew a thousand men therewith.

[16] And Samson said, With the jawbone of an ass, heaps upon heaps, with the jaw of an ass have I slain a thousand men.

Question: There are only two perfect cubes described in the Bible. Where are they?

Answer: The Most Holy Place and New Jerusalem

References: 1 Kings 6:16-20 and Revelation 21:10-16

(1 Kings 16-20)

[16] And he built twenty cubits on the sides of the house, both the floor and the walls with boards of cedar: he even built them for it within, even for the oracle, even for the most holy place.

[17] And the house, that is, the temple before it, was forty cubits long.

[18] And the cedar of the house within was carved with knops and open flowers: all was cedar; there was no stone seen.

[19] And the oracle he prepared in the house within, to set there the ark of the covenant of the Lord.

[20] And the oracle in the forepart was twenty cubits in length, and twenty cubits in breadth, and twenty cubits in the height thereof: and he overlaid it with pure gold; and so covered the altar which was of cedar.

(Revelation 21:10-16)

[10] And he carried me away in the spirit to a great and high mountain, and shewed me that great city, the holy Jerusalem, descending out of heaven from God,

[11] Having the glory of God: and her light was like unto a stone most precious, even like a jasper stone, clear as crystal;

[12] And had a wall great and high, and had twelve gates, and at the gates twelve angels, and names written thereon, which are the names of the twelve tribes of the children of Israel:

[13] On the east three gates; on the north three gates; on the south three gates; and on the west three gates.

[14] And the wall of the city had twelve foundations, and in them the names of the twelve apostles of the Lamb.

[15] And he that talked with me had a golden reed to measure the city, and the gates thereof, and the wall thereof.

[16] And the city lieth foursquare, and the length is as large as the breadth: and he

measured the city with the reed, twelve thousand furlongs. The length and the breadth and the height of it are equal.*

Question: What creatures brought Elijah bread and meat to eat during the drought?

Answer: Ravens

Reference: 1 Kings 17:2-6

(1 Kings 17:2-6)

[2] And the word of the Lord came unto him, saying,

[3] Get thee hence, and turn thee eastward, and hide thyself by the brook Cherith, that is before Jordan.

[4] And it shall be, that thou shalt drink of the brook; and I have commanded the ravens to feed thee there.

[5] So he went and did according unto the word of the Lord: for he went and dwelt by the brook Cherith, that is before Jordan.

[6] And the ravens brought him bread and flesh in the morning, and bread and flesh in the evening; and he drank of the brook.

Question: What test did Elijah put before the prophets of Baal that proved their gods were false?

Answer: He tasked the prophets of Baal to appeal to their gods to light a fire under their offering. When no fire ignited, it proved their god was false.

Reference: 1 Kings 18:22-39

(1 Kings 18:22-39)

[22] Then said Elijah unto the people, I, even I only, remain a prophet of the Lord; but Baal's prophets are four hundred and fifty men.

[23] Let them therefore give us two bullocks; and let them choose one bullock for themselves, and cut it in pieces, and lay it on wood, and put no fire under: and I will dress the other bullock, and lay it on wood, and put no fire under:

[24] And call ye on the name of your gods, and I will call on the name of the Lord: and the God that answereth by fire, let him be God. And all the people answered and said, It is well spoken.

[25] And Elijah said unto the prophets of Baal, Choose you one bullock for yourselves, and dress it first; for ye are many; and call on the name of your gods, but put no fire under.

[26] And they took the bullock which was given them, and they dressed it, and called on the name of Baal from morning even until noon, saying, O Baal, hear us. But there was no voice, nor any that answered. And they leaped upon the altar which was made.

[27] And it came to pass at noon, that Elijah mocked them, and said, Cry aloud: for he is a god; either he is talking, or he is pursuing, or he is in a journey, or peradventure he sleepeth, and must be awaked.

[28] And they cried aloud, and cut themselves after their manner with knives and lancets, till the blood gushed out upon them.

[29] And it came to pass, when midday was past, and they prophesied until the time of the offering of the evening sacrifice, that there was neither voice, nor any to answer, nor any that regarded.

[30] And Elijah said unto all the people, Come near unto me. And all the people came near unto him. And he repaired the altar of the Lord that was broken down.

[31] And Elijah took twelve stones, according to the number of the tribes of the sons of Jacob, unto whom the word of the Lord came, saying, Israel shall be thy name:

[32] And with the stones he built an altar in the name of the Lord: and he made a trench about the altar, as great as would contain two measures of seed.

[33] And he put the wood in order, and cut the bullock in pieces, and laid him on the wood, and said, Fill four barrels with water, and pour it on the burnt sacrifice, and on the wood.

[34] And he said, Do it the second time. And they did it the second time. And he said, Do it the third time. And they did it the third time.

[35] And the water ran round about the altar; and he filled the trench also with water.

[36] And it came to pass at the time of the offering of the evening sacrifice, that Elijah the prophet came near, and said, Lord God of

Abraham, Isaac, and of Israel, let it be known this day that thou art God in Israel, and that I am thy servant, and that I have done all these things at thy word.

[37] Hear me, O Lord, hear me, that this people may know that thou art the Lord God, and that thou hast turned their heart back again.

[38] Then the fire of the Lord fell, and consumed the burnt sacrifice, and the wood, and the stones, and the dust, and licked up the water that was in the trench.

[39] And when all the people saw it, they fell on their faces: and they said, The Lord, he is the God; the Lord, he is the God.

Question: Which King took possession of Naboth's vineyard?

Answer: Ahab

Reference: 1 Kings 21:13-16

(1 Kings 21:13-16)

[13] And there came in two men, children of Belial, and sat before him: and the men of Belial witnessed against him, even against Naboth, in the presence of the people, saying, Naboth did blaspheme God and the king. Then they carried him forth out of the city, and stoned him with stones, that he died.

[14] Then they sent to Jezebel, saying, Naboth is stoned, and is dead.

[15] And it came to pass, when Jezebel heard that Naboth was stoned, and was dead,

that Jezebel said to Ahab, Arise, take possession of the vineyard of Naboth the Jezreelite, which he refused to give thee for money: for Naboth is not alive, but dead.

[16] And it came to pass, when Ahab heard that Naboth was dead, that Ahab rose up to go down to the vineyard of Naboth the Jezreelite, to take possession of it.

Bible Fact: The Bible was written in three languages: Hebrew, Aramaic, and Greek.

Question: Who told Naaman to wash in the river Jordan seven times in order to cure his leprosy?

Answer: Elisha

Reference: 2 Kings 5:6-10

(2 Kings 5:6-10)

[6] And he brought the letter to the king of Israel, saying, Now when this letter is come unto thee, behold, I have therewith sent Naaman my servant to thee, that thou mayest recover him of his leprosy.

[7] And it came to pass, when the king of Israel had read the letter, that he rent his clothes, and said, Am I God, to kill and to make alive, that this man doth send unto me to recover a man of his leprosy? wherefore consider, I pray you, and see how he seeketh a quarrel against me.

[8] And it was so, when Elisha the man of God had heard that the king of Israel had rent

his clothes, that he sent to the king, saying, Wherefore hast thou rent thy clothes? let him come now to me, and he shall know that there is a prophet in Israel.

[9] So Naaman came with his horses and with his chariot, and stood at the door of the house of Elisha.

[10] And Elisha sent a messenger unto him, saying, Go and wash in Jordan seven times, and thy flesh shall come again to thee, and thou shalt be clean.

Bible Fact: The Bible is world's bestselling book. It has sold over 5 billion copies. In addition, more than 100 million copies of the Bible are sold each year.

Question: What punishment was given to Gehazi for his greed?

Answer: He was made leprous

Reference: 2 Kings 5:20-27

(2 Kings 5:20-27)

[20] But Gehazi, the servant of Elisha the man of God, said, Behold, my master hath spared Naaman this Syrian, in not receiving at his hands that which he brought: but, as the Lord liveth, I will run after him, and take somewhat of him.

[21] So Gehazi followed after Naaman. And when Naaman saw him running after him, he lighted down from the chariot to meet him, and said, Is all well?

[22] And he said, All is well. My master hath sent me, saying, Behold, even now there be come to me from mount Ephraim two young men of the sons of the prophets: give them, I pray thee, a talent of silver, and two changes of garments.

[23] And Naaman said, Be content, take two talents. And he urged him, and bound two talents of silver in two bags, with two changes of garments, and laid them upon two of his servants; and they bare them before him.

[24] And when he came to the tower, he took them from their hand, and bestowed them in the house: and he let the men go, and they departed.

[25] But he went in, and stood before his master. And Elisha said unto him, Whence comest thou, Gehazi? And he said, Thy servant went no whither.

[26] And he said unto him, Went not mine heart with thee, when the man turned again from his chariot to meet thee? Is it a time to receive money, and to receive garments, and oliveyards, and vineyards, and sheep, and oxen, and menservants, and maidservants?

[27] The leprosy therefore of Naaman shall cleave unto thee, and unto thy seed for ever. And he went out from his presence a leper as white as snow.

Question: Which two chapters of the Bible are identical?

Answer: 2 Kings 19 and Isaiah 37

Reference: 2 Kings 19 and Isaiah 37

(2 Kings 19 and Isaiah 37)

[1] And it came to pass, when king Hezekiah heard it, that he rent his clothes, and covered himself with sackcloth, and went into the house of the Lord.

[2] And he sent Eliakim, which was over the household, and Shebna the scribe, and the elders of the priests, covered with sackcloth, to Isaiah the prophet the son of Amoz.

[3] And they said unto him, Thus saith Hezekiah, This day is a day of trouble, and of rebuke, and blasphemy; for the children are come to the birth, and there is not strength to bring forth.

[4] It may be the Lord thy God will hear all the words of Rabshakeh, whom the king of Assyria his master hath sent to reproach the living God; and will reprove the words which the Lord thy God hath heard: wherefore lift up thy prayer for the remnant that are left.

[5] So the servants of king Hezekiah came to Isaiah.

[6] And Isaiah said unto them, Thus shall ye say to your master, Thus saith the Lord, Be not afraid of the words which thou hast heard, with which the servants of the king of Assyria have blasphemed me.

[7] Behold, I will send a blast upon him, and he shall hear a rumour, and shall return to his own land; and I will cause him to fall by the sword in his own land.

[8] So Rabshakeh returned, and found the king of Assyria warring against Libnah: for he had heard that he was departed from Lachish.

[9] And when he heard say of Tirhakah king of Ethiopia, Behold, he is come out to fight against thee: he sent messengers again unto Hezekiah, saying,

[10] Thus shall ye speak to Hezekiah king of Judah, saying, Let not thy God in whom thou trustest deceive thee, saying, Jerusalem shall not be delivered into the hand of the king of Assyria.

[11] Behold, thou hast heard what the kings of Assyria have done to all lands, by destroying them utterly: and shalt thou be delivered?

[12] Have the gods of the nations delivered them which my fathers have destroyed; as Gozan, and Haran, and Rezeph, and the children of Eden which were in Thelasar?

[13] Where is the king of Hamath, and the king of Arpad, and the king of the city of Sepharvaim, of Hena, and Ivah?

[14] And Hezekiah received the letter of the hand of the messengers, and read it: and Hezekiah went up into the house of the Lord, and spread it before the Lord.

[15] And Hezekiah prayed before the Lord, and said, O Lord God of Israel, which dwellest between the cherubims, thou art the God, even thou alone, of all the kingdoms of the earth; thou hast made heaven and earth.

[16] Lord, bow down thine ear, and hear: open, Lord, thine eyes, and see: and hear the words of Sennacherib, which hath sent him to reproach the living God.

[17] Of a truth, Lord, the kings of Assyria have destroyed the nations and their lands,

[18] And have cast their gods into the fire: for they were no gods, but the work of men's hands, wood and stone: therefore they have destroyed them.

[19] Now therefore, O Lord our God, I beseech thee, save thou us out of his hand, that all the kingdoms of the earth may know that thou art the Lord God, even thou only.

[20] Then Isaiah the son of Amoz sent to Hezekiah, saying, Thus saith the Lord God of Israel, That which thou hast prayed to me against Sennacherib king of Assyria I have heard.

[21] This is the word that the Lord hath spoken concerning him; The virgin the daughter of Zion hath despised thee, and laughed thee to scorn; the daughter of Jerusalem hath shaken her head at thee.

[22] Whom hast thou reproached and blasphemed? and against whom hast thou exalted thy voice, and lifted up thine eyes on high? even against the Holy One of Israel.

[23] By thy messengers thou hast reproached the Lord, and hast said, With the multitude of my chariots I am come up to the height of the mountains, to the sides of Lebanon, and will cut down the tall cedar

trees thereof, and the choice fir trees thereof: and I will enter into the lodgings of his borders, and into the forest of his Carmel.

[24] I have digged and drunk strange waters, and with the sole of my feet have I dried up all the rivers of besieged places.

[25] Hast thou not heard long ago how I have done it, and of ancient times that I have formed it? now have I brought it to pass, that thou shouldest be to lay waste fenced cities into ruinous heaps.

[26] Therefore their inhabitants were of small power, they were dismayed and confounded; they were as the grass of the field, and as the green herb, as the grass on the house tops, and as corn blasted before it be grown up.

[27] But I know thy abode, and thy going out, and thy coming in, and thy rage against me.

[28] Because thy rage against me and thy tumult is come up into mine ears, therefore I will put my hook in thy nose, and my bridle in thy lips, and I will turn thee back by the way by which thou camest.

[29] And this shall be a sign unto thee, Ye shall eat this year such things as grow of themselves, and in the second year that which springeth of the same; and in the third year sow ye, and reap, and plant vineyards, and eat the fruits thereof.

[30] And the remnant that is escaped of the house of Judah shall yet again take root downward, and bear fruit upward.

[31] For out of Jerusalem shall go forth a remnant, and they that escape out of mount Zion: the zeal of the Lord of hosts shall do this.

[32] Therefore thus saith the Lord concerning the king of Assyria, He shall not come into this city, nor shoot an arrow there, nor come before it with shield, nor cast a bank against it.

[33] By the way that he came, by the same shall he return, and shall not come into this city, saith the Lord.

[34] For I will defend this city, to save it, for mine own sake, and for my servant David's sake.

[35] And it came to pass that night, that the angel of the Lord went out, and smote in the camp of the Assyrians an hundred fourscore and five thousand: and when they arose early in the morning, behold, they were all dead corpses.

[36] So Sennacherib king of Assyria departed, and went and returned, and dwelt at Nineveh.

[37] And it came to pass, as he was worshipping in the house of Nisroch his god, that Adrammelech and Sharezer his sons smote him with the sword: and they escaped into the land of Armenia. And Esarhaddon his son reigned in his stead.

Question: How many troops did Sennacherib lose at the siege of Jerusalem?

Answer: 185,000

Reference: 2 Kings 19:32-36

(2 Kings 19:32-36)

[32] Therefore thus saith the Lord concerning the king of Assyria, He shall not come into this city, nor shoot an arrow there, nor come before it with shield, nor cast a bank against it.

[33] By the way that he came, by the same shall he return, and shall not come into this city, saith the Lord.

[34] For I will defend this city, to save it, for mine own sake, and for my servant David's sake.

[35] And it came to pass that night, that the angel of the Lord went out, and smote in the camp of the Assyrians an hundred fourscore and five thousand: and when they arose early in the morning, behold, they were all dead corpses.

[36] So Sennacherib king of Assyria departed, and went and returned, and dwelt at Nineveh.

Question: Which king decreed that the Jews could return to their land to rebuild the temple in Jerusalem?

Answer: Cyrus

Source: Ezra 1:1-4

(Ezra 1:1-4)

[1] Now in the first year of Cyrus king of Persia, that the word of the Lord by the mouth of Jeremiah might be fulfilled, the Lord stirred up the spirit of Cyrus king of Persia, that he made a proclamation throughout all his kingdom, and put it also in writing, saying,

[2] Thus saith Cyrus king of Persia, The Lord God of heaven hath given me all the kingdoms of the earth; and he hath charged me to build him an house at Jerusalem, which is in Judah.

[3] Who is there among you of all his people? his God be with him, and let him go up to Jerusalem, which is in Judah, and build the house of the Lord God of Israel, (he is the God,) which is in Jerusalem.

[4] And whosoever remaineth in any place where he sojourneth, let the men of his place help him with silver, and with gold, and with goods, and with beasts, beside the freewill offering for the house of God that is in Jerusalem.

Question: Who was king when the temple in Jerusalem was finished?

Answer: Darius

Source: Ezra 6:14-15

(Ezra 6:14-15)

[14] And the elders of the Jews builded, and they prospered through the prophesying of Haggai the prophet and Zechariah the son of

Iddo. And they builded, and finished it, according to the commandment of the God of Israel, and according to the commandment of Cyrus, and Darius, and Artaxerxes king of Persia.

[15] And this house was finished on the third day of the month Adar, which was in the sixth year of the reign of Darius the king.

Question: What service did Nehemiah perform for King Artaxerxes?

Answer: He was the king's cupbearer.

Source: Nehemiah 1:11

(Nehemiah 1:11)

[11] O Lord, I beseech thee, let now thine ear be attentive to the prayer of thy servant, and to the prayer of thy servants, who desire to fear thy name: and prosper, I pray thee, thy servant this day, and grant him mercy in the sight of this man. For I was the king's cupbearer.

Question: By what other name was Esther known?

Answer: Hadassah

Source: Esther 2:7

(Esther 2:7)

[7] And he brought up Hadassah, that is, Esther, his uncle's daughter: for she had neither father nor mother, and the maid was fair and beautiful; whom Mordecai, when her

father and mother were dead, took for his own daughter.

Question: Who made Esther the Queen of Persia?

Answer: King Ahasuerus

Source: Esther 2:16-17

(Esther 2:16-17)

[16] So Esther was taken unto king Ahasuerus into his house royal in the tenth month, which is the month Tebeth, in the seventh year of his reign.

[17] And the king loved Esther above all the women, and she obtained grace and favour in his sight more than all the virgins; so that he set the royal crown upon her head, and made her queen instead of Vashti.

Question: How many words are in longest verse of the King James Version of the Bible (Esther 8:9)?

Answer: 90

Source: Esther 8:9

(Esther 8:9)

[9] Then were the king's scribes called at that time in the third month, that is, the month Sivan, on the three and twentieth day thereof; and it was written according to all that Mordecai commanded unto the Jews, and to the lieutenants, and the deputies and rulers of the provinces which are from India unto

Ethiopia, an hundred twenty and seven provinces, unto every province according to the writing thereof, and unto every people after their language, and to the Jews according to their writing, and according to their language.

Question: Whom did God describe as "a perfect and an upright man"?

Answer: Job

Source: Job 1:7-8

(Job 1:7-8)

[7] And the Lord said unto Satan, Whence comest thou? Then Satan answered the Lord, and said, From going to and fro in the earth, and from walking up and down in it.

[8] And the Lord said unto Satan, Hast thou considered my servant Job, that there is none like him in the earth, a perfect and an upright man, one that feareth God, and escheweth evil?

Bible Fact: The first complete English translation of the Bible was by English theologian, Priest, and politician, John Wycliffe in 1382.

Question: When they heard of the adversity that had befallen Job, how many of his friends came to comfort him?

Answer: 3 (Eliphaz, Bildad, and Zophar)

Source: Job 2:11

(Job 2:11)

[11] Now when Job's three friends heard of all this evil that was come upon him, they came every one from his own place; Eliphaz the Temanite, and Bildad the Shuhite, and Zophar the Naamathite: for they had made an appointment together to come to mourn with him and to comfort him.

Question: What colors were the four horses of Revelation?

Answer: White, Red, Black, and Gray

Source: Revelation 6:1-8

(Revelation 6:1-8)

[1] And I saw when the Lamb opened one of the seals, and I heard, as it were the noise of thunder, one of the four beasts saying, Come and see.

[2] And I saw, and behold a white horse: and he that sat on him had a bow; and a crown was given unto him: and he went forth conquering, and to conquer.

[3] And when he had opened the second seal, I heard the second beast say, Come and see.

[4] And there went out another horse that was red: and power was given to him that sat thereon to take peace from the earth, and that they should kill one another: and there was given unto him a great sword.

[5] And when he had opened the third seal, I heard the third beast say, Come and see. And I beheld, and lo a black horse; and he that sat on him had a pair of balances in his hand.

[6] And I heard a voice in the midst of the four beasts say, A measure of wheat for a penny, and three measures of barley for a penny; and see thou hurt not the oil and the wine.

[7] And when he had opened the fourth seal, I heard the voice of the fourth beast say, Come and see.

[8] And I looked, and behold a pale horse: and his name that sat on him was Death, and Hell followed with him. And power was given unto them over the fourth part of the earth, to kill with sword, and with hunger, and with death, and with the beasts of the earth.

Question: "The Lord is my Shepherd", is the opening line to which Psalm?

Answer: The 23rd Psalm

Source: Psalm 23

(Psalm 23)

[1] The Lord is my shepherd; I shall not want.

[2] He maketh me to lie down in green pastures: he leadeth me beside the still waters.

[3] He restoreth my soul: he leadeth me in the paths of righteousness for his name's sake.

[4] Yea, though I walk through the valley of the shadow of death, I will fear no evil: for thou art with me; thy rod and thy staff they comfort me.

[5] Thou preparest a table before me in the presence of mine enemies: thou anointest my head with oil; my cup runneth over.

[6] Surely goodness and mercy shall follow me all the days of my life: and I will dwell in the house of the Lord for ever.

Bible Fact: The word "bible" is taken from the Greek *ta biblia*, which means "the scrolls" or "the books."

Question: What king made the law against praying?

Answer: King Darius

Source: Daniel 6:4-9

(Daniel 6:4-9)

[4] Then the presidents and princes sought to find occasion against Daniel concerning the kingdom; but they could find none occasion nor fault; forasmuch as he was faithful, neither was there any error or fault found in him.

[5] Then said these men, We shall not find any occasion against this Daniel, except we find it against him concerning the law of his God.

[6] Then these presidents and princes assembled together to the king, and said thus unto him, King Darius, live for ever.

[7] All the presidents of the kingdom, the governors, and the princes, the counsellors, and the captains, have consulted together to establish a royal statute, and to make a firm decree, that whosoever shall ask a petition of any God or man for thirty days, save of thee, O king, he shall be cast into the den of lions.

[8] Now, O king, establish the decree, and sign the writing, that it be not changed, according to the law of the Medes and Persians, which altereth not.

[9] Wherefore king Darius signed the writing and the decree.

Question: How many beasts did Daniel see in his dream?

Answer: 4

Source: Daniel 7:1-7

(Daniel 7:1-7)

[1] In the first year of Belshazzar king of Babylon Daniel had a dream and visions of his head upon his bed: then he wrote the dream, and told the sum of the matters.

[2] Daniel spake and said, I saw in my vision by night, and, behold, the four winds of the heaven strove upon the great sea.

[3] And four great beasts came up from the sea, diverse one from another.

[4] The first was like a lion, and had eagle's wings: I beheld till the wings thereof were plucked, and it was lifted up from the earth, and made stand upon the feet as a man, and a man's heart was given to it.

[5] And behold another beast, a second, like to a bear, and it raised up itself on one side, and it had three ribs in the mouth of it between the teeth of it: and they said thus unto it, Arise, devour much flesh.

[6] After this I beheld, and lo another, like a leopard, which had upon the back of it four wings of a fowl; the beast had also four heads; and dominion was given to it.

[7] After this I saw in the night visions, and behold a fourth beast, dreadful and terrible, and strong exceedingly; and it had great iron teeth: it devoured and brake in pieces, and stamped the residue with the feet of it: and it was diverse from all the beasts that were before it; and it had ten horns.

Question: Which city did Jonah try to flee to instead of going to Nineveh as God had commanded?

Answer: Tarshish

Source: Jonah 1:1-3

(John 1:1-3)

[1] Now the word of the Lord came unto Jonah the son of Amittai, saying,

[2] Arise, go to Nineveh, that great city, and cry against it; for their wickedness is come up before me.

[3] But Jonah rose up to flee unto Tarshish from the presence of the Lord, and went down to Joppa; and he found a ship going to Tarshish: so he paid the fare thereof, and went down into it, to go with them unto Tarshish from the presence of the Lord.

Question: How long was Jonah stuck inside the great fish?

Answer: 3 days

Source: Jonah 1:15, 17

(Jonah 1:15, 17)

[15] So they took up Jonah, and cast him forth into the sea: and the sea ceased from her raging.

[17] Now the Lord had prepared a great fish to swallow up Jonah. And Jonah was in the belly of the fish three days and three nights.

Bible Fact: In 1525, William Tyndale produced first printed edition of the New Testament in English.

Quote: "A thorough knowledge of the Bible is worth more than a college education." – Theodore Roosevelt

Question: In which town did the prophets state that the Messiah would be born?

Answer: Bethlehem

Source: Micah 5:2-4

Micah 5:2-4

[2] But thou, Bethlehem Ephratah, though thou be little among the thousands of Judah, yet out of thee shall he come forth unto me that is to be ruler in Israel; whose goings forth have been from of old, from everlasting.

[3] Therefore will he give them up, until the time that she which travaileth hath brought forth: then the remnant of his brethren shall return unto the children of Israel.

[4] And he shall stand and feed in the strength of the Lord, in the majesty of the name of the Lord his God; and they shall abide: for now shall he be great unto the ends of the earth.

Question: How is the name "Emmanuel" interpreted?

Answer: "God is with us"

Source: Matthew 1:21-23

(Matthew 1:21-23)

[21] And she shall bring forth a son, and thou shalt call his name Jesus: for he shall save his people from their sins.

[22] Now all this was done, that it might be fulfilled which was spoken of the Lord by the prophet, saying,

[23] Behold, a virgin shall be with child, and shall bring forth a son, and they shall call his name Emmanuel, which being interpreted is, God with us.

Bible Fact: Moses authored the first five books of the Old Testament.

Question: Where was Jesus born?

Answer: Bethlehem

Source: Matthew 2:1- 8

(Matthew 2:1-8)

[1] Now when Jesus was born in Bethlehem of Judaea in the days of Herod the king, behold, there came wise men from the east to Jerusalem,

[2] Saying, Where is he that is born King of the Jews? for we have seen his star in the east, and are come to worship him.

[3] When Herod the king had heard these things, he was troubled, and all Jerusalem with him.

[4] And when he had gathered all the chief priests and scribes of the people together, he demanded of them where Christ should be born.

[5] And they said unto him, In Bethlehem of Judaea: for thus it is written by the prophet,

[6] And thou Bethlehem, in the land of Juda, art not the least among the princes of Juda:

for out of thee shall come a Governor, that shall rule my people Israel.

[7] Then Herod, when he had privily called the wise men, enquired of them diligently what time the star appeared.

[8] And he sent them to Bethlehem, and said, Go and search diligently for the young child; and when ye have found him, bring me word again, that I may come and worship him also.

Question: How did King Herod the Great attempt to prevent Jesus from becoming king?

Answer: Herod ordered Jesus killed.

Source: Matthew 2:16-18

(Matthew 2:16-18)

[16] Then Herod, when he saw that he was mocked of the wise men, was exceeding wroth, and sent forth, and slew all the children that were in Bethlehem, and in all the coasts thereof, from two years old and under, according to the time which he had diligently inquired of the wise men.

[17] Then was fulfilled that which was spoken by Jeremiah the prophet, saying,

[18] In Rama was there a voice heard, lamentation, and weeping, and great mourning, Rachel weeping for her children, and would not be comforted, because they are not.

Bible Fact: Paul wrote over half of the books of the New Testament. He authored 14 of the 27 New Testament books.

Question: Of what did the diet of John the Baptist subsist?

Answer: Locusts and wild honey

Source: Matthew 3:4

(Matthew 3:4)

[4] And the same John had his raiment of camel's hair, and a leathern girdle about his loins; and his meat was locusts and wild honey.

Question: How many Beatitudes are listed in the Book of Matthew?

Answer: 9

Source: Matthew 5:1-11

(Matthew 5:1-11)

[1] And seeing the multitudes, he went up into a mountain: and when he was set, his disciples came unto him:

[2] And he opened his mouth, and taught them, saying,

[3] Blessed are the poor in spirit: for theirs is the kingdom of heaven.

[4] Blessed are they that mourn: for they shall be comforted.

[5] Blessed are the meek: for they shall inherit the earth.

[6] Blessed are they which do hunger and thirst after righteousness: for they shall be filled.

[7] Blessed are the merciful: for they shall obtain mercy.

[8] Blessed are the pure in heart: for they shall see God.

[9] Blessed are the peacemakers: for they shall be called the children of God.

[10] Blessed are they which are persecuted for righteousness' sake: for theirs is the kingdom of heaven.

[11] Blessed are ye, when men shall revile you, and persecute you, and shall say all manner of evil against you falsely, for my sake.

Bible Fact: The Geneva Bible was the first Bible to use numbered verses. The Pilgrims brought the Geneva Bible with them to North America in 1620.

Question: According to the words of Jesus in the Sermon on the Mount, "a city that is on a hill cannot be" what?

Answer: Hidden

Source: Matthew 5:14

(Matthew 5:14)
[14] Ye are the light of the world. A city that is set on an hill cannot be hid.

Question: How many words are in Lord's Prayer according to the Book of Matthew in the King James Version of the Bible (including the word "Amen")?

Answer: 66

Source: Matthew 6:9-13

(Matthew 6:9-13)

[9] . . . Our Father which art in heaven, Hallowed be thy name.

[10] Thy kingdom come, Thy will be done in earth, as it is in heaven.

[11] Give us this day our daily bread.

[12] And forgive us our debts, as we forgive our debtors.

[13] And lead us not into temptation, but deliver us from evil: For thine is the kingdom, and the power, and the glory, for ever. Amen.

Bible Fact: Thieves steal more Bibles each year than any other book.

Question: Which of the 12 main Disciples was a tax collector?

Answer: Matthew (Aka Levi)

Source: Matthew 9:9

(Matthew 9:9)

[9] And as Jesus passed forth from thence, he saw a man, named Matthew, sitting at the receipt of custom: and he saith unto him, Follow me. And he arose, and followed him.

Question: In the parable of the sower, what happened to the seeds that fell by the wayside?

Answer: Birds devoured them.

Source: Matthew 13:3-4

(Matthew 13:3-4)

[3] And he spake many things unto them in parables, saying, Behold, a sower went forth to sow;

[4] And when he sowed, some seeds fell by the way side, and the fowls came and devoured them up:

Question: What was the fate of John the Baptist?

Answer: Herod Antipas first had him arrested and then ordered him beheaded.

Source: Matthew 14:3-12

(Matthew 14:3-12)

[3] For Herod had laid hold on John, and bound him, and put him in prison for Herodias' sake, his brother Philip's wife.

[4] For John said unto him, It is not lawful for thee to have her.

[5] And when he would have put him to death, he feared the multitude, because they counted him as a prophet.

[6] But when Herod's birthday was kept, the daughter of Herodias danced before them, and pleased Herod.

[7] Whereupon he promised with an oath to give her whatsoever she would ask.

[8] And she, being before instructed of her mother, said, Give me here John Baptist's head in a charger.

[9] And the king was sorry: nevertheless for the oath's sake, and them which sat with him at meat, he commanded it to be given her.

[10] And he sent, and beheaded John in the prison.

[11] And his head was brought in a charger, and given to the damsel: and she brought it to her mother.

[12] And his disciples came, and took up the body, and buried it, and went and told Jesus.

Bible Fact: In 1782, Robert Aitken's Bible (The King James Version without the Apocrypha) became the first English language Bible printed in the United States.

Question: What did Jesus use to feed the 5,000?

Answer: 5 loaves and 2 fish

Source: Matthew 14:13-21

(Matthew 14:13-21)

[13] When Jesus heard of it, he departed thence by ship into a desert place apart: and when the people had heard thereof, they followed him on foot out of the cities.

[14] And Jesus went forth, and saw a great multitude, and was moved with compassion toward them, and he healed their sick.

[15] And when it was evening, his disciples came to him, saying, This is a desert place, and the time is now past; send the multitude away, that they may go into the villages, and buy themselves victuals.

[16] But Jesus said unto them, They need not depart; give ye them to eat.

[17] And they say unto him, We have here but five loaves, and two fishes.

[18] He said, Bring them hither to me.

[19] And he commanded the multitude to sit down on the grass, and took the five loaves, and the two fishes, and looking up to heaven, he blessed, and brake, and gave the loaves to his disciples, and the disciples to the multitude.

[20] And they did all eat, and were filled: and they took up of the fragments that remained twelve baskets full.

[21] And they that had eaten were about five thousand men, beside women and children.

Quote: "I've read the last page of the Bible; it's all going to turn out all right." – Billy Graham

Question: On which Sea did Jesus perform the miracle of walking on water?

Answer: The Sea of Galilee

Source: Matthew 14:22-27

(Matthew 14:22-27)

[22] And straightway Jesus constrained his disciples to get into a ship, and to go before him unto the other side, while he sent the multitudes away.

[23] And when he had sent the multitudes away, he went up into a mountain apart to pray: and when the evening was come, he was there alone.

[24] But the ship was now in the midst of the sea, tossed with waves: for the wind was contrary.

[25] And in the fourth watch of the night Jesus went unto them, walking on the sea.

[26] And when the disciples saw him walking on the sea, they were troubled, saying, It is a spirit; and they cried out for fear.

[27] But straightway Jesus spake unto them, saying, Be of good cheer; it is I; be not afraid.

Question: What did Jesus use to feed the 4,000?

Answer: Seven loafs of bread and a few fish

Source: Matthew 15:30-38

(Matthew 15:30-38)

[30] And great multitudes came unto him, having with them those that were lame, blind,

dumb, maimed, and many others, and cast them down at Jesus' feet; and he healed them:

[31] Insomuch that the multitude wondered, when they saw the dumb to speak, the maimed to be whole, the lame to walk, and the blind to see: and they glorified the God of Israel.

[32] Then Jesus called his disciples unto him, and said, I have compassion on the multitude, because they continue with me now three days, and have nothing to eat: and I will not send them away fasting, lest they faint in the way.

[33] And his disciples say unto him, Whence should we have so much bread in the wilderness, as to fill so great a multitude?

[34] And Jesus saith unto them, How many loaves have ye? And they said, Seven, and a few little fishes.

[35] And he commanded the multitude to sit down on the ground.

[36] And he took the seven loaves and the fishes, and gave thanks, and brake them, and gave to his disciples, and the disciples to the multitude.

[37] And they did all eat, and were filled: and they took up of the broken meat that was left seven baskets full.

[38] And they that did eat were four thousand men, beside women and children.

Question: Which three Disciples were present at the transfiguration?

Answer: Peter, James, and John

Source: Matthew 17:1-8

(Matthew 17:1-8)

[1] And after six days Jesus taketh Peter, James, and John his brother, and bringeth them up into an high mountain apart,

[2] And was transfigured before them: and his face did shine as the sun, and his raiment was white as the light.

[3] And, behold, there appeared unto them Moses and Elias talking with him.

[4] Then answered Peter, and said unto Jesus, Lord, it is good for us to be here: if thou wilt, let us make here three tabernacles; one for thee, and one for Moses, and one for Elias.

[5] While he yet spake, behold, a bright cloud overshadowed them: and behold a voice out of the cloud, which said, This is my beloved Son, in whom I am well pleased; hear ye him.

[6] And when the disciples heard it, they fell on their face, and were sore afraid.

[7] And Jesus came and touched them, and said, Arise, and be not afraid.

[8] And when they had lifted up their eyes, they saw no man, save Jesus only.

Question: What did Jesus send Disciples to fetch before his triumphal entry into Jerusalem?

Answer: A donkey and a colt

Source: Matthew 21:1-5

(Matthew 21:1-5)

[1] And when they drew nigh unto Jerusalem, and were come to Bethphage, unto the mount of Olives, then sent Jesus two disciples,

[2] Saying unto them, Go into the village over against you, and straightway ye shall find an ass tied, and a colt with her: loose them, and bring them unto me.

[3] And if any man say ought unto you, ye shall say, The Lord hath need of them; and straightway he will send them.

[4] All this was done, that it might be fulfilled which was spoken by the prophet, saying,

[5] Tell ye the daughter of Sion, Behold, thy King cometh unto thee, meek, and sitting upon an ass, and a colt the foal of an ass.

Question: In the parable of the ten virgins, what were they waiting for?

Answer: The Bridegroom

Source: Matthew 25:1-10

(Matthew 25:1-10)

[1] Then shall the kingdom of heaven be likened unto ten virgins, which took their lamps, and went forth to meet the bridegroom.

[2] And five of them were wise, and five were foolish.

[3] They that were foolish took their lamps, and took no oil with them:

[4] But the wise took oil in their vessels with their lamps.

[5] While the bridegroom tarried, they all slumbered and slept.

[6] And at midnight there was a cry made, Behold, the bridegroom cometh; go ye out to meet him.

[7] Then all those virgins arose, and trimmed their lamps.

[8] And the foolish said unto the wise, Give us of your oil; for our lamps are gone out.

[9] But the wise answered, saying, Not so; lest there be not enough for us and you: but go ye rather to them that sell, and buy for yourselves.

[10] And while they went to buy, the bridegroom came; and they that were ready went in with him to the marriage: and the door was shut.

Bible Fact: The events depicted in the Bible take place across three continents: Asia, Africa, and Europe.

Question: Who met to conspire to capture and then to murder Jesus?

Answer: The chief priests, scribes, elders of the people, and the high priest, Caiaphas.

Source: Matthew 26:1-5

(Matthew 26:1-5)

[1] And it came to pass, when Jesus had finished all these sayings, he said unto his disciples,

[2] Ye know that after two days is the feast of the passover, and the Son of man is betrayed to be crucified.

[3] Then assembled together the chief priests, and the scribes, and the elders of the people, unto the palace of the high priest, who was called Caiaphas,

[4] And consulted that they might take Jesus by subtilty, and kill him.

[5] But they said, Not on the feast day, lest there be an uproar among the people.

Bible Fact: Johannes Gutenberg produced the first printed version of the Bible in 1454.

Question: What payment did Judas accept for betraying Jesus?

Answer: 30 pieces of silver

Source: Matthew 26:14-16

(Matthew 26:14-16)

[14] Then one of the twelve, called Judas Iscariot, went unto the chief priests,

[15] And said unto them, What will ye give me, and I will deliver him unto you? And they covenanted with him for thirty pieces of silver.

[16] And from that time he sought opportunity to betray him.

Question: To which garden did Jesus go and pray in before his arrest?

Answer: Gethsemane

Source: Matthew 26:36-39

(Matthew 26:36-39)

[36] Then cometh Jesus with them unto a place called Gethsemane, and saith unto the disciples, Sit ye here, while I go and pray yonder.

[37] And he took with him Peter and the two sons of Zebedee, and began to be sorrowful and very heavy.

[38] Then saith he unto them, My soul is exceeding sorrowful, even unto death: tarry ye here, and watch with me.

[39] And he went a little farther, and fell on his face, and prayed, saying, O my Father, if it be possible, let this cup pass from me: nevertheless not as I will, but as thou wilt.

Question: What became of Judas Iscariot?

Answer: He hanged himself.

Source: Matthew 27:5

(Matthew 27:5)

[1] When the morning was come, all the chief priests and elders of the people took counsel against Jesus to put him to death:

[2] And when they had bound him, they led him away, and delivered him to Pontius Pilate the governor.

[3] Then Judas, which had betrayed him, when he saw that he was condemned, repented himself, and brought again the thirty pieces of silver to the chief priests and elders,

[4] Saying, I have sinned in that I have betrayed the innocent blood. And they said, What is that to us? see thou to that.

[5] And he cast down the pieces of silver in the temple, and departed, and went and hanged himself.

Question: Whom did the crowd vote to release instead of Jesus?

Answer: Barabbas

Source: Matthew 27:15-22

(Matthew 27:15-22)

[15] Now at that feast the governor was wont to release unto the people a prisoner, whom they would.

[16] And they had then a notable prisoner, called Barabbas.

[17] Therefore when they were gathered together, Pilate said unto them, Whom will ye that I release unto you? Barabbas, or Jesus which is called Christ?

[18] For he knew that for envy they had delivered him.

[19] When he was set down on the judgment seat, his wife sent unto him, saying, Have thou nothing to do with that just man: for I have

suffered many things this day in a dream because of him.

[20] But the chief priests and elders persuaded the multitude that they should ask Barabbas, and destroy Jesus.

[21] The governor answered and said unto them, Whether of the twain will ye that I release unto you? They said, Barabbas.

[22] Pilate saith unto them, What shall I do then with Jesus which is called Christ? They all say unto him, Let him be crucified.

Bible Fact: Malachi, authored about 400 B.C., was the last Old Testament book written.

Question: According to the King James Version of the Bible, what does "Golgotha" mean?

Answer: "a place of a skull"

Source: Matthew 27:33-34

(Matthew 27:33-34)

[33] And when they were come unto a place called Golgotha, that is to say, a place of a skull,

[34] They gave him vinegar to drink mingled with gall: and when he had tasted thereof, he would not drink.

Question: What part of the day did Jesus embark on the boat from which He calmed the waters?

Answer: Evening

Reference: Mark 4:3541

(Mark 4:35-41)

[35] *And the same day, when the even was come, he saith unto them, Let us pass over unto the other side.*

[36] *And when they had sent away the multitude, they took him even as he was in the ship. And there were also with him other little ships.*

[37] *And there arose a great storm of wind, and the waves beat into the ship, so that it was now full.*

[38] *And he was in the hinder part of the ship, asleep on a pillow: and they awake him, and say unto him, Master, carest thou not that we perish?*

[39] *And he arose, and rebuked the wind, and said unto the sea, Peace, be still. And the wind ceased, and there was a great calm.*

[40] *And he said unto them, Why are ye so fearful? how is it that ye have no faith?*

[41] *And they feared exceedingly, and said one to another, What manner of man is this, that even the wind and the sea obey him?*

Question: The High Priest Melchizedek was also ruled what city?

Answer: Salem (Jerusalem)

Reference: Genesis 14:18-20

(Genesis 14:18)

[18] And Melchizedek king of Salem brought forth bread and wine: and he was the priest of the most high God.

[19] And he blessed him, and said, Blessed be Abram of the most high God, possessor of heaven and earth:

[20] And blessed be the most high God, which hath delivered thine enemies into thy hand. And he gave him tithes of all.

Question: About how many swine did Jesus send the unclean spirits into when he ordered them out of the tormented man?

Answer: 2,000

Source: Mark 5:1-13

(Mark 5:1-13)

[1] And they came over unto the other side of the sea, into the country of the Gadarenes.

[2] And when he was come out of the ship, immediately there met him out of the tombs a man with an unclean spirit,

[3] Who had his dwelling among the tombs; and no man could bind him, no, not with chains:

[4] Because that he had been often bound with fetters and chains, and the chains had been plucked asunder by him, and the fetters broken in pieces: neither could any man tame him.

[5] And always, night and day, he was in the mountains, and in the tombs, crying, and cutting himself with stones.

[6] But when he saw Jesus afar off, he ran and worshipped him,

[7] And cried with a loud voice, and said, What have I to do with thee, Jesus, thou Son of the most high God? I adjure thee by God, that thou torment me not.

[8] For he said unto him, Come out of the man, thou unclean spirit.

[9] And he asked him, What is thy name? And he answered, saying, My name is Legion: for we are many.

[10] And he besought him much that he would not send them away out of the country.

[11] Now there was there nigh unto the mountains a great herd of swine feeding.

[12] And all the devils besought him, saying, Send us into the swine, that we may enter into them.

[13] And forthwith Jesus gave them leave. And the unclean spirits went out, and entered into the swine: and the herd ran violently down a steep place into the sea, (they were about two thousand;) and were choked in the sea.

Question: An angel told Zacharias and Elizabeth they would have a son. What did the angel say the child's name would be?

Answer: John

Source: Luke 1:5-17

(Luke 1:5-17)

[5] There was in the days of Herod, the king of Judaea, a certain priest named Zacharias, of the course of Abia: and his wife was of the daughters of Aaron, and her name was Elisabeth.

[6] And they were both righteous before God, walking in all the commandments and ordinances of the Lord blameless.

[7] And they had no child, because that Elisabeth was barren, and they both were now well stricken in years.

[8] And it came to pass, that while he executed the priest's office before God in the order of his course,

[9] According to the custom of the priest's office, his lot was to burn incense when he went into the temple of the Lord.

[10] And the whole multitude of the people were praying without at the time of incense.

[11] And there appeared unto him an angel of the Lord standing on the right side of the altar of incense.

[12] And when Zacharias saw him, he was troubled, and fear fell upon him.

[13] But the angel said unto him, Fear not, Zacharias: for thy prayer is heard; and thy wife Elisabeth shall bear thee a son, and thou shalt call his name John.

[14] And thou shalt have joy and gladness; and many shall rejoice at his birth.

[15] For he shall be great in the sight of the Lord, and shall drink neither wine nor strong drink; and he shall be filled with the Holy Ghost, even from his mother's womb.

[16] And many of the children of Israel shall he turn to the Lord their God.

[17] And he shall go before him in the spirit and power of Elias, to turn the hearts of the fathers to the children, and the disobedient to the wisdom of the just; to make ready a people prepared for the Lord.

Question: What punishment did Zacharias receive for not believing the angel?

Answer: He lost the ability to speak

Reference: Luke 1:18-22

(Luke 1:18-22)

[18] And Zacharias said unto the angel, Whereby shall I know this? for I am an old man, and my wife well stricken in years.

[19] And the angel answering said unto him, I am Gabriel, that stand in the presence of God; and am sent to speak unto thee, and to shew thee these glad tidings.

[20] And, behold, thou shalt be dumb, and not able to speak, until the day that these things shall be performed, because thou believest not my words, which shall be fulfilled in their season.

[21] And the people waited for Zacharias, and marvelled that he tarried so long in the temple.

[22] And when he came out, he could not speak unto them: and they perceived that he had seen a vision in the temple: for he beckoned unto them, and remained speechless.

Question: Who decreed the taking of a census of the entire Roman at the time of Jesus' birth?

Answer: Augustus Caesar

Reference: Luke 2:1-3

(Luke 2:1)

[1] And it came to pass in those days, that there went out a decree from Caesar Augustus that all the world should be taxed.

[2] (And this taxing was first made when Cyrenius was governor of Syria.)

[3] And all went to be taxed, every one into his own city.

Question: What happened to Jesus on the 8th day of his life?

Answer: He was circumcised and he was named Jesus.

Source: Luke 2:21-24

(Luke 2:21-24)

[21] And when eight days were accomplished for the circumcising of the child,

his name was called Jesus, which was so named of the angel before he was conceived in the womb.

[22] And when the days of her purification according to the law of Moses were accomplished, they brought him to Jerusalem, to present him to the Lord;

[23] (As it is written in the law of the Lord, Every male that openeth the womb shall be called holy to the Lord;)

[24] And to offer a sacrifice according to that which is said in the law of the Lord, A pair of turtledoves, or two young pigeons.

Bible Fact: Complete versions of the Bible have been translated into more than 500 languages. Partial versions of the Bible have been translated into more than 2,800 languages.

Question: At the age of 12, Jesus was left behind in Jerusalem. Where did his parents find him?

Answer: In the temple, sitting in the midst of the doctors, both hearing them, and asking them questions.

Source: Luke 2:40-49

(Luke 2:40-49)

[40] And the child grew, and waxed strong in spirit, filled with wisdom: and the grace of God was upon him.

[41] Now his parents went to Jerusalem every year at the feast of the passover.

[42] And when he was twelve years old, they went up to Jerusalem after the custom of the feast.

[43] And when they had fulfilled the days, as they returned, the child Jesus tarried behind in Jerusalem; and Joseph and his mother knew not of it.

[44] But they, supposing him to have been in the company, went a day's journey; and they sought him among their kinsfolk and acquaintance.

[45] And when they found him not, they turned back again to Jerusalem, seeking him.

[46] And it came to pass, that after three days they found him in the temple, sitting in the midst of the doctors, both hearing them, and asking them questions.

[47] And all that heard him were astonished at his understanding and answers.

[48] And when they saw him, they were amazed: and his mother said unto him, Son, why hast thou thus dealt with us? behold, thy father and I have sought thee sorrowing.

[49] And he said unto them, How is it that ye sought me? wist ye not that I must be about my Father's business?

Question: What form did the Holy Spirit take at the baptism of Jesus?

Answer: A dove

Source: Luke 3:21-22

(Luke 3:21-22)

[21] Now when all the people were baptized, it came to pass, that Jesus also being baptized, and praying, the heaven was opened,

[22] And the Holy Ghost descended in a bodily shape like a dove upon him, and a voice came from heaven, which said, Thou art my beloved Son; in thee I am well pleased.

Question: In the parable of the Good Samaritan, who were the two persons that passed by the robbed man?

Answer: A Priest and a Levite

Source: Luke 10:30-34

(Luke 10:30-34)

[30] And Jesus answering said, A certain man went down from Jerusalem to Jericho, and fell among thieves, which stripped him of his raiment, and wounded him, and departed, leaving him half dead.

[31] And by chance there came down a certain priest that way: and when he saw him, he passed by on the other side.

[32] And likewise a Levite, when he was at the place, came and looked on him, and passed by on the other side.

[33] But a certain Samaritan, as he journeyed, came where he was: and when he saw him, he had compassion on him,

[34] And went to him, and bound up his wounds, pouring in oil and wine, and set him on his own beast, and brought him to an inn, and took care of him.

Question: What job did the Prodigal Son take after squandering his inheritance?

Answer: He became a pig feeder

Reference: Luke 15:14-15

(Luke 15:14-15)

]14] And when he had spent all, there arose a mighty famine in that land; and he began to be in want.

[15] And he went and joined himself to a citizen of that country; and he sent him into his fields to feed swine.

Question: Where did Jesus find Zacchaeus, the chief tax collector?

Answer: Up a tree

Source: Luke 19:1-6

(Luke 19:1-6)

[1] And Jesus entered and passed through Jericho.

[2] And, behold, there was a man named Zacchaeus, which was the chief among the publicans, and he was rich.

[3] And he sought to see Jesus who he was; and could not for the press, because he was little of stature.

[4] And he ran before, and climbed up into a sycomore tree to see him: for he was to pass that way.

[5] And when Jesus came to the place, he looked up, and saw him, and said unto him, Zacchaeus, make haste, and come down; for to day I must abide at thy house.

[6] And he made haste, and came down, and received him joyfully.

Question: Which Disciple denied Jesus three times?

Answer: Peter

Source: Luke 22:54-62

(Luke 22:54-62)

[54] Then took they him, and led him, and brought him into the high priest's house. And Peter followed afar off.

[55] And when they had kindled a fire in the midst of the hall, and were set down together, Peter sat down among them.

[56] But a certain maid beheld him as he sat by the fire, and earnestly looked upon him, and said, This man was also with him.

[57] And he denied him, saying, Woman, I know him not.

[58] And after a little while another saw him, and said, Thou art also of them. And Peter said, Man, I am not.

[59] And about the space of one hour after another confidently affirmed, saying, Of a

truth this fellow also was with him: for he is a Galilaean.

[60] And Peter said, Man, I know not what thou sayest. And immediately, while he yet spake, the cock crew.

[61] And the Lord turned, and looked upon Peter. And Peter remembered the word of the Lord, how he had said unto him, Before the cock crow, thou shalt deny me thrice.

[62] And Peter went out, and wept bitterly.

Question: The sounding of fifth trumpet in Revelation caused a plague similar to a plague placed upon Egypt in the Book of Exodus. Which one?

Answer: The Plague of Locusts

Source: Revelation 9:1-10

(Revelation 9:1-10)

[1] And the fifth angel sounded, and I saw a star fall from heaven unto the earth: and to him was given the key of the bottomless pit.

[2] And he opened the bottomless pit; and there arose a smoke out of the pit, as the smoke of a great furnace; and the sun and the air were darkened by reason of the smoke of the pit.

[3] And there came out of the smoke locusts upon the earth: and unto them was given power, as the scorpions of the earth have power.

[4] And it was commanded them that they should not hurt the grass of the earth, neither any green thing, neither any tree; but only those men which have not the seal of God in their foreheads.

[5] And to them it was given that they should not kill them, but that they should be tormented five months: and their torment was as the torment of a scorpion, when he striketh a man.

[6] And in those days shall men seek death, and shall not find it; and shall desire to die, and death shall flee from them.

[7] And the shapes of the locusts were like unto horses prepared unto battle; and on their heads were as it were crowns like gold, and their faces were as the faces of men.

[8] And they had hair as the hair of women, and their teeth were as the teeth of lions.

[9] And they had breastplates, as it were breastplates of iron; and the sound of their wings was as the sound of chariots of many horses running to battle.

[10] And they had tails like unto scorpions, and there were stings in their tails: and their power was to hurt men five months.

Quote: "Nobody ever outgrows scripture; the book widens and deepens with our years." – Charles Spurgeon

Question: What miracle did Jesus perform at the marriage in Cana?

Answer: He turned water into wine.

Source: John 2:1-11

(John 2:1-11)

[1] And the third day there was a marriage in Cana of Galilee; and the mother of Jesus was there:

[2] And both Jesus was called, and his disciples, to the marriage.

[3] And when they wanted wine, the mother of Jesus saith unto him, They have no wine.

[4] Jesus saith unto her, Woman, what have I to do with thee? mine hour is not yet come.

[5] His mother saith unto the servants, Whatsoever he saith unto you, do it.

[6] And there were set there six waterpots of stone, after the manner of the purifying of the Jews, containing two or three firkins apiece.

[7] Jesus saith unto them, Fill the waterpots with water. And they filled them up to the brim.

[8] And he saith unto them, Draw out now, and bear unto the governor of the feast. And they bare it.

[9] When the ruler of the feast had tasted the water that was made wine, and knew not whence it was: (but the servants which drew the water knew;) the governor of the feast called the bridegroom,

[10] And saith unto him, Every man at the beginning doth set forth good wine; and when

men have well drunk, then that which is worse: but thou hast kept the good wine until now.

[11] This beginning of miracles did Jesus in Cana of Galilee, and manifested forth his glory; and his disciples believed on him.

Question: How long is the shortest verse of the King James Version of the Bible?

Answer: Two words

Source: John 11:35

(John 11:35)

[35] Jesus wept.

Question: What was the name of the servant of the High Priest who had his ear cut off at the arrest of Jesus?

Answer: Malchus

Source: John 18:10-11

(John 18:10-11)

[10] Then Simon Peter having a sword drew it, and smote the high priest's servant, and cut off his right ear. The servant's name was Malchus.

[11] Then said Jesus unto Peter, Put up thy sword into the sheath: the cup which my Father hath given me, shall I not drink it?

Question: What did Thomas want to see before he would believe that Jesus had been raised from the dead?

Answer: Jesus' wounds

Source: John 20:24-29

(John 20:24-29)

[24] But Thomas, one of the twelve, called Didymus, was not with them when Jesus came.

[25] The other disciples therefore said unto him, We have seen the Lord. But he said unto them, Except I shall see in his hands the print of the nails, and put my finger into the print of the nails, and thrust my hand into his side, I will not believe.

[26] And after eight days again his disciples were within, and Thomas with them: then came Jesus, the doors being shut, and stood in the midst, and said, Peace be unto you.

[27] Then saith he to Thomas, Reach hither thy finger, and behold my hands; and reach hither thy hand, and thrust it into my side: and be not faithless, but believing.

[28] And Thomas answered and said unto him, My Lord and my God.

[29] Jesus saith unto him, Thomas, because thou hast seen me, thou hast believed: blessed are they that have not seen, and yet have believed.

Bible Fact: The People's Republic of China manufactures more Bibles than any other country in the world. Ironically, the government of the People's Republic of China is officially atheist.

Question: Why did John write his Gospel?

Answer: ". . .that ye might believe that Jesus is the Christ, the Son of God; and that believing ye might have life through his name."

Source: John 20:30-31

(John 20:30-31)

[30] And many other signs truly did Jesus in the presence of his disciples, which are not written in this book:

[31] But these are written, that ye might believe that Jesus is the Christ, the Son of God; and that believing ye might have life through his name.

Bible Fact: The first authorized Bible printed in English is the Great Bible of 1539. King Henry VIII of England proclaimed that it be read aloud during services conducted by clergymen of the Church of England.

Question: Where were the disciples first called Christians?

Answer: Antioch

Source: Acts 11:25-26

(Acts 11:25-26)

[25] Then departed Barnabas to Tarsus, for to seek Saul:

[26] And when he had found him, he brought him unto Antioch. And it came to pass, that a whole year they assembled themselves with the church, and taught much people. And the disciples were called Christians first in Antioch.

Question: Which founder of a Gnostic religious sect received mention in the New Testament?

Answer: Simon Magus

Source: Acts 8:9-24

(Acts 8:9-24)

[9] But there was a certain man, called Simon, which beforetime in the same city used sorcery, and bewitched the people of Samaria, giving out that himself was some great one:

[10] To whom they all gave heed, from the least to the greatest, saying, This man is the great power of God.

[11] And to him they had regard, because that of long time he had bewitched them with sorceries.

[12] But when they believed Philip preaching the things concerning the kingdom of God, and the name of Jesus Christ, they were baptized, both men and women.

[13] Then Simon himself believed also: and when he was baptized, he continued with Philip, and wondered, beholding the miracles and signs which were done.

[14] Now when the apostles which were at Jerusalem heard that Samaria had received the word of God, they sent unto them Peter and John:

[15] Who, when they were come down, prayed for them, that they might receive the Holy Ghost:

[16] (For as yet he was fallen upon none of them: only they were baptized in the name of the Lord Jesus.)

[17] Then laid they their hands on them, and they received the Holy Ghost.

[18] And when Simon saw that through laying on of the apostles' hands the Holy Ghost was given, he offered them money,

[19] Saying, Give me also this power, that on whomsoever I lay hands, he may receive the Holy Ghost.

[20] But Peter said unto him, Thy money perish with thee, because thou hast thought that the gift of God may be purchased with money.

[21] Thou hast neither part nor lot in this matter: for thy heart is not right in the sight of God.

[22] Repent therefore of this thy wickedness, and pray God, if perhaps the thought of thine heart may be forgiven thee.

[23] For I perceive that thou art in the gall of bitterness, and in the bond of iniquity.

[24] Then answered Simon, and said, Pray ye to the Lord for me, that none of these things which ye have spoken come upon me.

Question: What was the name of the special container designed specifically to hold God's commandments?

Answer: The Ark of the Covenant

Source: Hebrews 9:3-5

(Hebrews 9:3-5)

[3] And after the second veil, the tabernacle which is called the Holiest of all;

[4] Which had the golden censer, and the ark of the covenant overlaid round about with gold, wherein was the golden pot that had manna, and Aaron's rod that budded, and the tables of the covenant;

[5] And over it the cherubims of glory shadowing the mercyseat; of which we cannot now speak particularly.

Bible Fact: Adam's name is from the Hebrew term *a da ma*, which means "the ground."

Quote: "There are more sure marks of authenticity in the Bible than in any profane history." – Isaac Newton

Question: How many people were sealed as "servants of our God on their forehead"?

Answer: 144,000

Source: Revelation 7:4

(Revelation 7:4)

[3] Saying, Hurt not the earth, neither the sea, nor the trees, till we have sealed the servants of our God in their foreheads.

[4] And I heard the number of them which were sealed: and there were sealed an hundred and forty and four thousand of all the tribes of the children of Israel.

Question: What are the final words of Jesus recorded in the New Testament?

Answer: "Surely I come quickly."

Source: Revelation 22:18-20

(Revelation 22:18-20)

[18] For I testify unto every man that heareth the words of the prophecy of this book, If any man shall add unto these things, God shall add unto him the plagues that are written in this book:

[19] And if any man shall take away from the words of the book of this prophecy, God shall take away his part out of the book of life, and out of the holy city, and from the things which are written in this book.

[20] He which testifieth these things saith, Surely I come quickly. Amen. Even so, come, Lord Jesus.

Bible Fact: The word "Christ" is from the Greek term *khristos*, meaning "the anointed."

Question: Who did Mary think Jesus was at first after the resurrection?

Answer: A gardener

Source: John 20:11-16

(John 20:11-16)

[11] But Mary stood without at the sepulchre weeping: and as she wept, she stooped down, and looked into the sepulchre,

[12] And seeth two angels in white sitting, the one at the head, and the other at the feet, where the body of Jesus had lain.

[13] And they say unto her, Woman, why weepest thou? She saith unto them, Because they have taken away my Lord, and I know not where they have laid him.

[14] And when she had thus said, she turned herself back, and saw Jesus standing, and knew not that it was Jesus.

[15] Jesus saith unto her, Woman, why weepest thou? whom seekest thou? She, supposing him to be the gardener, saith unto him, Sir, if thou have borne him hence, tell me where thou hast laid him, and I will take him away.

[16] Jesus saith unto her, Mary. She turned herself, and saith unto him, Rabboni; which is to say, Master.

Bible Fact: The most expensive book in the world is "The Bay Psalm Book." It once sold for more than $14 million. It was the first book printed America.

Question: Which group of people stood and watched Jesus as he ascended into heaven?

Answer: Men of Galilee (The Disciples)

Source: Acts 1:9-11

(Acts 1:9-11)

[9] And when he had spoken these things, while they beheld, he was taken up; and a cloud received him out of their sight.

[10] And while they looked stedfastly toward heaven as he went up, behold, two men stood by them in white apparel;

[11] Which also said, Ye men of Galilee, why stand ye gazing up into heaven? this same Jesus, which is taken up from you into heaven, shall so come in like manner as ye have seen him go into heaven.

Question: On what day did the apostles receive the Holy Spirit?

Answer: The day of Pentecost

Source: Acts 2:1-4

(Acts 2:1-4)

[1] And when the day of Pentecost was fully come, they were all with one accord in one place.

[2] And suddenly there came a sound from heaven as of a rushing mighty wind, and it filled all the house where they were sitting.

[3] And there appeared unto them cloven tongues like as of fire, and it sat upon each of them.

[4] And they were all filled with the Holy Ghost, and began to speak with other tongues, as the Spirit gave them utterance.

Question: What did Peter and John heal the man of at the temple gate called Beautiful?

Answer: Lameness

Source: Acts 3:1-2

(Acts 3:1-8)

[1] Now Peter and John went up together into the temple at the hour of prayer, being the ninth hour.

[2] And a certain man lame from his mother's womb was carried, whom they laid daily at the gate of the temple which is called Beautiful, to ask alms of them that entered into the temple;

[3] Who seeing Peter and John about to go into the temple asked an alms.

[4] And Peter, fastening his eyes upon him with John, said, Look on us.

[5] And he gave heed unto them, expecting to receive something of them.

[6] Then Peter said, Silver and gold have I none; but such as I have give I thee: In the name of Jesus Christ of Nazareth rise up and walk.

[7] And he took him by the right hand, and lifted him up: and immediately his feet and ankle bones received strength.

[8] And he leaping up stood, and walked, and entered with them into the temple, walking, and leaping, and praising God.

Question: Whom did God send to restore Saul's (Paul's) sight?

Answer: Ananias

Source: Acts 9:17-18

(Acts 9:8-18)

[8] And Saul arose from the earth; and when his eyes were opened, he saw no man: but they led him by the hand, and brought him into Damascus.

[9] And he was three days without sight, and neither did eat nor drink.

[10] And there was a certain disciple at Damascus, named Ananias; and to him said the Lord in a vision, Ananias. And he said, Behold, I am here, Lord.

[11] And the Lord said unto him, Arise, and go into the street which is called Straight, and enquire in the house of Judas for one called Saul, of Tarsus: for, behold, he prayeth,

[12] And hath seen in a vision a man named Ananias coming in, and putting his hand on him, that he might receive his sight.

[13] Then Ananias answered, Lord, I have heard by many of this man, how much evil he hath done to thy saints at Jerusalem:

[14] And here he hath authority from the chief priests to bind all that call on thy name.

[15] But the Lord said unto him, Go thy way: for he is a chosen vessel unto me, to bear my name before the Gentiles, and kings, and the children of Israel:

[16] For I will shew him how great things he must suffer for my name's sake.

[17] And Ananias went his way, and entered into the house; and putting his hands on him said, Brother Saul, the Lord, even Jesus, that appeared unto thee in the way as thou camest, hath sent me, that thou mightest receive thy sight, and be filled with the Holy Ghost.

[18] And immediately there fell from his eyes as it had been scales: and he received sight forthwith, and arose, and was baptized.

Question: Whom did Paul take with him on his first missionary journey?

Answer: Barnabas

Source: Acts 13:1-4

(Acts 13:1-4)

[1] Now there were in the church that was at Antioch certain prophets and teachers; as Barnabas, and Simeon that was called Niger, and Lucius of Cyrene, and Manaen, which had been brought up with Herod the tetrarch, and Saul.

[2] As they ministered to the Lord, and fasted, the Holy Ghost said, Separate me Barnabas and Saul for the work whereunto I have called them.

[3] And when they had fasted and prayed, and laid their hands on them, they sent them away.

[4] So they, being sent forth by the Holy Ghost, departed unto Seleucia; and from thence they sailed to Cyprus.

Question: What event occurred to help release Paul and Silas from prison?

Answer: An earthquake

Reference: Acts 16:26

(Acts 16:26)

[26] And suddenly there was a great earthquake, so that the foundations of the prison were shaken: and immediately all the doors were opened, and every one's bands were loosed.

[27] And the keeper of the prison awaking out of his sleep, and seeing the prison doors open, he drew out his sword, and would have killed himself, supposing that the prisoners had been fled.

[28] But Paul cried with a loud voice, saying, Do thyself no harm: for we are all here.

[29] Then he called for a light, and sprang in, and came trembling, and fell down before Paul and Silas,

[30] And brought them out, and said, Sirs, what must I do to be saved?

[31] And they said, Believe on the Lord Jesus Christ, and thou shalt be saved, and thy house.

[32] And they spake unto him the word of the Lord, and to all that were in his house.

[33] And he took them the same hour of the night, and washed their stripes; and was baptized, he and all his, straightway.

[34] And when he had brought them into his house, he set meat before them, and rejoiced, believing in God with all his house.

[35] And when it was day, the magistrates sent the serjeants, saying, Let those men go.

[36] And the keeper of the prison told this saying to Paul, The magistrates have sent to let you go: now therefore depart, and go in peace.

Question: What was the last word of the King James Version of the Bible?

Answer: Amen

Source: Revelation: 22:21

(Revelation: 22:21)

[21] The grace of our Lord Jesus Christ be with you all. Amen.

Conclusion

It is our sincere hope that you have enjoyed this book and that you will reference it in the future. It is also our hope that you will read the Bible and accept the gifts that it has to offer.

If you would like to comment on this book, or converse about the Bible, you can contact us by email at clgammon@hotmail.com or you can write us at:

CL and Kim Gammon

3312 Scottsville, RD

Lafayette, TN 37083

May God Bless you.

About the Authors

Kim Gammon has studied the Bible for many years. She includes Bible trivia in the weekly church bulletin she prepares as part of her duties as Secretary and Social Media representative for her local church. She attends Volunteer State Community College. This is her first book.

CL Gammon has had a life-long fascination with American History and with the written word. These joint fascinations have led to his becoming an award winning and an internationally known bestselling author of more than thirty books. Gammon, who studied Political Science at Tennessee Technological University and History and Government at Hillsdale College, has entertained and educated readers for more than a decade. Several universities, including the State University of New York and the University of Akron, have used his books as course material. In addition, articles written by Gammon have appeared in more than a dozen publications.

Kim and CL Gammon live in Lafayette, Tennessee with their family.

Other Books by CL Gammon

CL Gammon has written books covering many topics including history, politics, sports, and fiction. They include:

Abraham Lincoln: Warrior in Chief

A Laughing Witch: Hanging Suzanna Martin

Alexander Hamilton's Plan for America

America's First Rules of War

America's Fourteen Presidents

America's Other Party: A Brief History of the Prohibition Party

A Revolutionary War Cookbook (And More)

Bad Football Saturday's 50 Worst Teams Ever!

Ballyhoo: John Butler and the Monkey Trial

Bizarre Murders in Tennessee: 13 True Stories

Dixie Witches: 9 True Southern Witch Trials

Expelling the Senate's Gentlemen Traitors

Guns, Politics and Independence

Hail to the Chief: The Presidency by the Numbers

Hanging the Macon County Witch

Jefferson Davis Rallies the Rebels (1863)

Make Sure You are Right, then Go Ahead and other Essays

McGovern-Eagleton '72: A Crazy Train Wreck

Nazi Mad Science I: High Altitude Experiments

Real Love Potions, Spells, and Charms

Salem Sends Its First Witch to the Gallows

Seven Candidates for President in 1972

Simon the Accuser: A Christian Novel

Squeaky & Sara Jane Try to Off Jerry Ford

The American Presidents: Briefly

The Big Fire (A novel)

The Continental Congress: America's Forgotten Government

The Great Mormon War of 1857-1858

The Great New Hampshire Primary Myth

The Hampton Roads Conference

The Macon County Race War

The Philosophy of the Confederate Constitution

The Politics of the Crucifixion

The Preamble of the United States Constitution

The Story of the First Continental Congress

The True Story of Axis Sally

Ultimate Penalty: Executing Robert Glen Coe

Ultimate Penalty II: Executing Sedley Alley

Was Lucille Ball a Communist?

Why Johnson Created the Warren Commission

Why the Articles of Confederation Failed

www.ingramcontent.com/pod-product-compliance
Lightning Source LLC
LaVergne TN
LVHW021808201224
799627LV00002B/222